POCKET POSTERS

GCSE **Maths**
Revision Guide

Improving understanding through colour and clarity

daydream®
EDUCATION

GCSE **Maths**

Number

Algebra

Contents

Maths Jargon

+	Addition	**4 + 3 = 7**
−	Subtraction	**7 − 5 = 2**
×	Multiplication	**2 × 4 = 8**
÷	Division	**12 ÷ 3 = 4**
=	Is equal to	$\frac{1}{2} = 0.5$
≠	Is not equal to	**3 ≠ 4**
≈	Approximate	**a ≈ 4,000**

Prime Numbers

2	17	5	19	67	13	79	19

Prime numbers have only 2 factors, themselves and 1.

Prime factors are factors which are also prime numbers. For example, 2 and 3 are prime factors of 12.

Factors

Every number has **factors**. The **factors** of **12** are **1, 2, 3, 4, 6** and **12** because all of these numbers go exactly into 12.

The **highest common factor (HCF)** of two numbers is the largest whole number which is a factor of both numbers.

The **HCF** of 18 and 30 is 6:

Factors of 18: 1, 2, 3, **6**, 9, 18

Factors of 30: 1, 2, 3, 5, **6**, 10, 15, 30

Multiples

Every number has **multiples**. For example, every number that 3 goes into is a **multiple** of 3, so **3, 6, 9, 12, 15, 18**... etc. are all multiples of 3.

The **lowest common multiple (LCM)** of two numbers is the smallest whole number which is a multiple of both numbers.

The **LCM** of 4 and 10 is 20:

Multiples of 4: 4, 8, 12, 16, **20**, 24

Multiples of 10: 10, **20**, 30, 40, 50

Squares & Cubes

1^2 2^2 3^2

$1 \times 1 = 1$ $2 \times 2 = 4$ $3 \times 3 = 9$

A **square number** is the product of a number multiplied by itself.

1^3 2^3 3^3

$1 \times 1 \times 1 = 1$ $2 \times 2 \times 2 = 8$ $3 \times 3 \times 3 = 27$

A **cube number** is the product of a number multiplied by itself 3 times.

Inequalities

1 < 3
1 is less than 3

3 > 1
3 is more than 1

≤ Less than or equal to
$y \leq 5$ *y* is less than or equal to 5

≥ More than or equal to
$y \geq 7$ *y* is more than or equal to 7

daydream
EDUCAT

Approximate

Not exact; close to the exact value. This often means rounding to a significant figure or decimal point.

Pi is approximately equal to 3.14. $\pi \approx 3.14$.

Convert

To change from one unit of measure to another.

If £1 = $0.9 convert £20 into dollars.

Calculate

To find the answer to a mathematical problem.

Calculate the cost of 10 apples when 1 apple costs 50p.

Estimate

To calculate an approximate value for a number. Usually, rounding each number within a calculation to a significant figure will make it easier.

$$\frac{31 \times 9.98}{0.46} \approx \frac{30 \times 10}{0.5} \approx \frac{300}{0.5} \approx 600$$

Evaluate

To work out the value of a numerical or algebraic expression.

Evaluate $x^2 + 1$ when $x = 2$.

Express

To represent or show something in a different form or way.

*15 out of 30 pupils passed their maths exam.
Express this as a percentage.*

Identify

To find, determine or establish the answer to something.

Identify how many sides and angles a square has.

Simplify

To make simpler. In maths, this can involve reducing a fraction to its simplest form or collecting algebraic expressions together.

$$3x + 5 + 2x - 4 \implies 5x + 1$$

Construct

To draw geometric shapes and angles.

Construct a right angle triangle using a compass and a rule.

Prove

To demonstrate, with evidence, that something is true.
A question may ask you to prove algebraically.

Prove that angles in the same segment and standing on the same chord are always equal.

Place Value

The value of each digit in a number depends upon its position or place. The position or place of **each digit** represents a power of ten.

Thousands 1000s	Hundreds 100s	Tens 10s	Ones 1s	Decimal Point	Tenths 1/10	Hundredths 1/100	Thousandths 1/1000
1	6	8	2	●	4	7	3
Whole numbers with a value of 0 or more					Numbers with a value of less than 1		

Look at what each digit in the numbers below represents.

324
is made up of:
3 hundreds
2 tens
4 ones

46
is made up of:
4 tens
6 ones

6457
is made up of:
6 thousands
4 hundreds
5 tens
7 ones

2.45
is made up of:
2 ones
4 tenths
5 hundredths

Look at the numbers below. What does the digit 4 in each number represent?
Can you put the numbers in order from smallest to largest?

34   426   748   8421   304   3.04   7.46

Adding and Subtracting by Powers of 10

To **increase** a number by **one thousand**, add one to the thousands digit.
$3482 + 1000 = 4482$

To **increase** a number by **one hundred**, add one to the hundreds digit.
$3482 + 100 = 3582$

To **increase** a number by **ten**, add one to the tens digit.
$3482 + 10 = 3492$

Thousands 1000s	Hundreds 100s	Tens 10s	Ones 1s
3	4	8	2

To **decrease** a number by **one thousand**, subtract one from the thousands digit.
$3482 - 1000 = 2482$

To **decrease** a number by **one hundred**, subtract one from the hundreds digit.
$3482 - 100 = 3382$

To **decrease** a number by **ten**, subtract one from the tens digit.
$3482 - 10 = 3472$

What happens if the digit you are adding to is 9?

If you add one to nine you get ten: $9 + 1 = 10$.
The same rule applies when adding other powers of 10.

To add 10 to 3492:
Add one to the hundreds digit and change the tens digit to zero.
$3492 + 10 = 3502$
You've gone from 49 tens to 50 tens.

To add 100 to 3982:
Add one to the thousands digit and change the hundreds digit to zero.
$3982 + 100 = 4082$
You've gone from 39 hundreds to 40 hundreds.

daydream EDUCATION

Negative Numbers

A negative number is any number that is less than zero. Negative numbers are denoted by a minus sign, **–**.

The number line below shows the integers, or whole numbers, from -10 to 10.

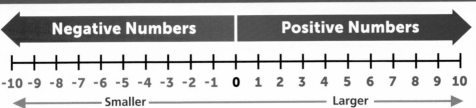

← **Negative Numbers** | **Positive Numbers** →

-10 -9 -8 -7 -6 -5 -4 -3 -2 -1 **0** 1 2 3 4 5 6 7 8 9 10

← Smaller ——— | ——— Larger →

Numbers to the **left** on a number line are smaller than those to their **right**. The value of negative numbers decreases from right to left. For example, –7 is less than –2.

Real-life examples of negative numbers include:

 **Temperature** | **Bank Balances**

The following rules apply when adding or subtracting negative numbers.

Adding a negative number is the same as subtracting. It produces a lower value.

$$2 \boxed{+ -3} = -1$$

+ –3

-2 -1 **0** 1 2 3

If you **add a** negative number, you move to the **left** on a number line.

Subtracting a negative number is the same as adding. It produces a higher value.

$$4 \boxed{- -2} = 6$$

– –2

3 4 5 6 7 8

If you **subtract a** negative number, you move to the **right** on a number line.

The following rules apply when multiplying or dividing negative numbers.

$$2 \times -3 = -6$$

Multiplying a positive number by a negative number (and vice versa) produces a negative number.

$$21 \div -3 = -7$$

Dividing a positive number by a negative number (and vice versa) produces a negative number.

$$-2 \times -3 = 6$$

Multiplying two negative numbers produces a positive number.

$$-18 \div -3 = 6$$

Dividing a negative number by a negative number produces a positive number.

---

daydream EDUCATION

9

Column Addition

It is not always possible to perform addition in your head. In such instances, column addition should be used.

To solve this addition problem, follow the steps outlined below.

$56 + 272 + 191$

1 List all numbers underneath one another, so that digits with the same place value (hundreds, tens, ones) are aligned vertically.

```
  h  t  o
     5  6
  2  7  2
+ 1  9  1
─────────
```

2 When performing column addition, always work from **right to left**.

Add the numbers in the ones column first.

$6 + 2 + 1 = 9$

Write the answer underneath the numbers that are being added together.

```
  h  t  o
     5  6
  2  7  2
+ 1  9  1
─────────
        9
```

3 Add the numbers in the tens column.

$5 + 7 + 9 = 21$

If the answer has two digits, the second digit, 1, is written underneath the numbers added in the tens column, and the first digit, 2, which represents 200, is carried over to the hundreds column.

Write the carried number here.

```
  h  t  o
     5  6
  2  7  2
+ 1  9  1
─────────
     1  9
  2
```

4 Add the numbers in the hundreds column, and remember to include any carried numbers.

$2 + 1 + 2$ (the carried number) $= 5$

Write the answer underneath the numbers that are being added together. The addition is now complete.

$56 + 272 + 191 = 519$

Remember to add me!

```
  h  t  o
     5  6
  2  7  2
+ 1  9  1
─────────
  5  1  9
  2
```

daydream
EDUCATIO

Column Subtraction

It is not always possible to perform subtraction in your head. In such instances, column subtraction should be used.

To solve this subtraction problem, follow the steps outlined below.

639 – 271

1 List the number being subtracted, 271, **under** the other number, 639, so that digits with the same place value (hundreds, tens, ones) are aligned vertically.

```
  h  t  o
  6  3  9
- 2  7  1
_____
```

2 When performing column subtraction, always work from **right to left**.

Subtract the numbers in the ones column first.

9 – 1 = **8**

Write the answer underneath the ones column.

```
  h  t  o
  6  3  9
- 2  7  1
_____
        8
```

3 Subtract the numbers in the tens column. If the top number is smaller than the bottom number, take 1 from the column to the left (hundreds).

More on the floor?
Go next door and get 10 more!

Because 3 is smaller than 7, take 1 from the hundreds column. The 6 in the hundreds column becomes 5, and the 3 in the tens column becomes 13.

13 – 7 = **6**

```
   h   t  o
  5ᵍ ¹3  9
-  2   7  1
_____
       6  8
```

4 Subtract the numbers in the hundreds column, and write the answer underneath.

5 – 2 = **3**

The subtraction is now complete.

639 – 271 = **368**

```
   h   t  o
  5ᵍ ¹3  9
-  2   7  1
_____
   3   6  8
```

Times Tables 1-6

One

1 × 1 = **1**
2 × 1 = 2
3 × 1 = 3
4 × 1 = 4
5 × 1 = 5
6 × 1 = 6
7 × 1 = 7
8 × 1 = 8
9 × 1 = 9
10 × 1 = 10
11 × 1 = 11
12 × 1 = 12

Two

1 × 2 = 2
2 × 2 = **4**
3 × 2 = 6
4 × 2 = 8
5 × 2 = 10
6 × 2 = 12
7 × 2 = 14
8 × 2 = 16
9 × 2 = 18
10 × 2 = 20
11 × 2 = 22
12 × 2 = 24

Three

1 × 3 = 3
2 × 3 = 6
3 × 3 = **9**
4 × 3 = 12
5 × 3 = 15
6 × 3 = 18
7 × 3 = 21
8 × 3 = 24
9 × 3 = 27
10 × 3 = 30
11 × 3 = 33
12 × 3 = 36

Four

1 × 4 = 4
2 × 4 = 8
3 × 4 = 12
4 × 4 = **16**
5 × 4 = 20
6 × 4 = 24
7 × 4 = 28
8 × 4 = 32
9 × 4 = 36
10 × 4 = 40
11 × 4 = 44
12 × 4 = 48

Five

1 × 5 = 5
2 × 5 = 10
3 × 5 = 15
4 × 5 = 20
5 × 5 = **25**
6 × 5 = 30
7 × 5 = 35
8 × 5 = 40
9 × 5 = 45
10 × 5 = 50
11 × 5 = 55
12 × 5 = 60

Six

1 × 6 = 6
2 × 6 = 12
3 × 6 = 18
4 × 6 = 24
5 × 6 = 30
6 × 6 = **36**
7 × 6 = 42
8 × 6 = 48
9 × 6 = 54
10 × 6 = 60
11 × 6 = 66
12 × 6 = 72

The numbers in orange are the ones you've already learnt.
If you look closely they have appeared in a previous table.

The numbers in boxes are called square numbers. Why?   4 × 4 = 16

12

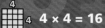

Times Tables 7-12

Seven

1 × 7 = 7
2 × 7 = 14
3 × 7 = 21
4 × 7 = 28
5 × 7 = 35
6 × 7 = 42
7 × 7 = 49
8 × 7 = 56
9 × 7 = 63
10 × 7 = 70
11 × 7 = 77
12 × 7 = 84

Eight

1 × 8 = 8
2 × 8 = 16
3 × 8 = 24
4 × 8 = 32
5 × 8 = 40
6 × 8 = 48
7 × 8 = 56
8 × 8 = 64
9 × 8 = 72
10 × 8 = 80
11 × 8 = 88
12 × 8 = 96

Nine

1 × 9 = 9
2 × 9 = 18
3 × 9 = 27
4 × 9 = 36
5 × 9 = 45
6 × 9 = 54
7 × 9 = 63
8 × 9 = 72
9 × 9 = 81
10 × 9 = 90
11 × 9 = 99
12 × 9 = 108

Ten

1 × 10 = 10
2 × 10 = 20
3 × 10 = 30
4 × 10 = 40
5 × 10 = 50
6 × 10 = 60
7 × 10 = 70
8 × 10 = 80
9 × 10 = 90
10 × 10 = 100
11 × 10 = 110
12 × 10 = 120

Eleven

1 × 11 = 11
2 × 11 = 22
3 × 11 = 33
4 × 11 = 44
5 × 11 = 55
6 × 11 = 66
7 × 11 = 77
8 × 11 = 88
9 × 11 = 99
10 × 11 = 110
11 × 11 = 121
12 × 11 = 132

Twelve

1 × 12 = 12
2 × 12 = 24
3 × 12 = 36
4 × 12 = 48
5 × 12 = 60
6 × 12 = 72
7 × 12 = 84
8 × 12 = 96
9 × 12 = 108
10 × 12 = 120
11 × 12 = 132
12 × 12 = 144

The numbers in orange are the ones you've already learnt.
If you look closely they have appeared in a previous table.

The numbers in boxes are called square numbers. Why?   8 × 8 = 64

Long Multiplication

It is not always possible to perform multiplication in your head. In such instances, long multiplication should be used.

To solve this multiplication problem, follow the steps outlined below.

232×6

1 Write the smaller number underneath the larger number, so that digits with the same place value (hundreds, tens, ones) are aligned vertically.

```
  h  t  o
  2  3  2
×        6
_____
```

2 Multiply each digit in the top number by the bottom number. Always work from **right to left**.

$2 \times 6 = 12$

Write the 2 underneath the ones column and carry the 1 over to the tens column.

Write the carried number here.

```
  h  t  o
  2  3  2
×        6
_____
         2
      1
```

3 Multiply the next digit, 3, in the top number by the bottom number, 6, and add any carried numbers.

$3 \times 6 = 18; 18 + 1 \text{ (the carried number)} = 19$

Write the 9 underneath the tens column and carry the 1 over to the hundreds column.

Remember to add me!

```
  h  t  o
  2  3  2
×        6
_____
      9  2
  1  1
```

4 Multiply the next digit, 2, in the top number by the bottom number, 6, and add any carried numbers.

$2 \times 6 = 12; 12 + 1 \text{ (the carried number)} = 13$

As there are no more numbers to multiply, the whole number can be written underneath. The multiplication problem is now solved.

$232 \times 6 = 1392$

```
  h  t  o
  2  3  2
×        6
_____
1  3  9  2
  1  1
```

14

daydream
EDUCATION

To solve this multiplication problem, follow the steps outlined below.

471 × 52

1
Rewrite the multiplication problem so that the smaller number is written under the larger number.

Multiply each digit in the top number by the bottom number. Always work from **right to left**.

$1 × 2 = 2$

Write the 2 underneath the ones column.

```
      h  t  o
      4  7  1
   ×     5  2
            2
```

2
Working from **right to left**, multiply the next digits in the top number by the bottom number, 2. Remember to add any carried numbers.

$7 × 2 = 14$
$4 × 2 = 8; 8 + 1$ (the carried number) $= 9$
Therefore, $2 × 471 = 942$

```
      h  t  o
      4  7  1
   ×     5  2
      9  4  2
      1
```

3
Before the top number can be multiplied by the next digit in the bottom number, 5, a zero needs to be added in the ones column. This is because the 5 in the bottom number actually represents 50.

It is **vital** that this step is performed or the answer will be incorrect.

```
      h  t  o
      4  7  1
   ×     5  2
      9  4  2
      1
            0
```

4
Now multiply each digit in the top number by 5. Remember to work **from right to left**.

$1 × 5 = 5$
$7 × 5 = 35$
$4 × 5 = 20; 20 + 3$ (the carried number) $= 23$
Therefore, $50 × 471 = 23,550$

```
       h  t  o
       4  7  1
    ×     5  2
       9  4  2
       1
  2  3  5  5  0
     3
```

5
Finally, use column addition to add the two products together.

$2 + 0 = 2$
$4 + 5 = 9$
$9 + 5 = 14$
$3 + 1$ (the carried number) $= 4$
2

Therefore, $471 × 52 = 24,492$

Do **not** include these numbers when adding up!

```
        h  t  o
        4  7  1
     ×     5  2
        9  4  2
          ①
  +  2  3  5  5  0
        ③
     2  4  4  9  2
              1
```

Short Division

To solve this division problem, follow the steps outlined below.

The number being divided is called the dividend. → $8192 \div 4$ ← The number by which the dividend is divided is called the divisor.

The answer to a division problem is called the **quotient**.

1 Rewrite the division problem so that the dividend (8192) is written in a division bracket and the divisor (4) is written to the left of the bracket.

$$4\overline{)8\ 1\ 9\ 2}$$

2 Short division is performed from left to right, so divide the first digit in the dividend (8) by the divisor (4).

4 goes into 8 twice: $8 \div 4 = 2$

Write 2 directly above the first digit in the dividend.

$$4\overline{)\overset{2}{8}\ 1\ 9\ 2}$$

3 Divide the next digit in the dividend by the divisor. In this instance, 4 does not go into 1. Therefore, 0 is written above the division bracket, and the 1 is carried over to the next digit (9) to create 19.

$$4\overline{)\overset{2\ 0}{8\ 1\ {}^19\ 2}}$$

4 Divide 19 by the divisor (4).

4 goes into 19 four times ($4 \times 4 = 16$) with 3 left over so:

$19 \div 4 = 4$ remainder 3

Write 4 above the 9 in the division bracket, and carry the remainder (3) over to the next digit (2) to create 32.

$$4\overline{)\overset{2\ 0\ 4}{8\ 1\ {}^19\ {}^32}}$$

5 Divide 32 by the divisor (4).

4 goes into 32 eight times so:

$32 \div 4 = 8$

Write 8 above the 2 in the dividend. The division problem is now complete.

$8192 \div 4 = 2048$

$$4\overline{)\overset{2\ 0\ 4\ 8}{8\ 1\ {}^19\ {}^32}}$$

daydream
EDUCATIO

Order of Operations

When calculations involve multiple operations, they must be performed in a specific order.

The acronym **BIDMAS** is used to remember the correct order of operation.

B Brackets	**Brackets** first	$(6 + 2)$
I Indices	Then **indices** or roots	3^2
D Division **M** Multiplication	Then **divide** or **multiply** in order from left to right	$\dfrac{2 \times 4}{3}$
A Addition **S** Subtraction	Finally, **add** or **subtract** in order from left to right	$3 + 6 - 2$

$4 + 2 \times 3$

$2 \times 3 = 6$
$4 + 6 = 10$

B ▶ none
I ▶ none
D or M ▶ $2 \times 3 = 6$
A or S ▶ $4 + 6 = 10$

$20 \div (3 + 2)$

$3 + 2 = 5$
$20 \div 5 = 4$

B ▶ $3 + 2 = 5$
I ▶ none
D or M ▶ $20 \div 5 = 4$
A or S ▶ none

$5 + 3^2 - 6 \times 4$

$3^2 = 9$
$6 \times 4 = 24$
$5 + 9 = 14$
$14 - 24 = -10$

B ▶ none
I ▶ $3^2 = 9$
D or M ▶ $6 \times 4 = 24$
A or S ▶ $5 + 9 = 14$
$14 - 24 = -10$

$6 - 2 + 4 - 3$

$6 - 2 = 4$
$4 + 4 = 8$
$8 - 3 = 5$

B ▶ none
I ▶ none
D or M ▶ none
A or S ▶ $6 - 2 = 4$
$4 + 4 = 8$
$8 - 3 = 5$

$(2^2 + 4)^2 \times 4$

$2^2 = 4$
$4 + 4 = 8$
$8^2 = 64$
$64 \times 4 = 256$

B ▶ $2^2 = 4$
$4 + 4 = 8$
I ▶ $8^2 = 64$
D or M ▶ $64 \times 4 = 256$
A or S ▶ none

Within brackets, order of operations still apply so indices are performed before addition.

$(3 + 8 \div 2)^2$

$8 \div 2 = 4$
$3 + 4 = 7$
$7^2 = 49$

B ▶ $8 \div 2 = 4$
$3 + 4 = 7$
I ▶ $7^2 = 49$
D or M ▶ none
A or S ▶ none

Within brackets, order of operations still apply so division is performed before addition.

Prime Numbers

A **prime number** is a whole number that has only **two** factors: itself and 1.

For example, **7** is a **prime number** because it has only **two** factors: 7 and 1.

$$7 \div 7 = 1 \quad \text{and} \quad 7 \div 1 = 7$$

1	2	3	4	5	6	7	8	9	10
11	12	13	14	15	16	17	18	19	20
21	22	23	24	25	26	27	28	29	30
31	32	33	34	35	36	37	38	39	40
41	42	43	44	45	46	47	48	49	50
51	52	53	54	55	56	57	58	59	60
61	62	63	64	65	66	67	68	69	70
71	72	73	74	75	76	77	78	79	80
81	82	83	84	85	86	87	88	89	90
91	92	93	94	95	96	97	98	99	100

13 is a prime number. It has **two** factors: 13 and 1.
$$13 \div 1 = 13 \quad 13 \div 13 = 1$$

1 is **not** a prime number. It has only **one** factor: 1.
$$1 \div 1 = 1$$

2 is the lowest and only even prime number. It has **two** factors: 2 and 1.
$$2 \div 1 = 2 \quad 2 \div 2 = 1$$

6 is **not** a prime number. It has **four** factors: 1, 2, 3 and 6.
$$6 \div 1 = 6 \quad 6 \div 2 = 3$$
$$6 \div 3 = 2 \quad 6 \div 6 = 1$$

daydream EDUCATION

Prime Factor Decomposition

Any number can be written as a **product of prime factors** - a string of prime numbers that when multiplied together, total the original number.

Factor Trees

A factor tree is used to find the prime factor decomposition of a number.

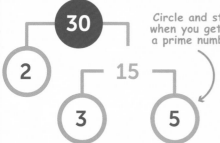

Circle and stop when you get to a prime number

$2 \times 3 \times 5 = 30$

1	Find a **factor pair** of 30. **2** and **15** are a factor pair of 30.
2	Find **factor pairs** of these numbers. **3** and **5** are a factor pair of 15. **2** is a prime number so cannot be broken down.
3	If possible, repeat the step above. **3** and **5** are prime numbers so cannot be broken down.

Express 261 as a product of prime factors.

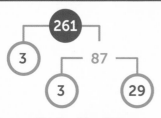

$3 \times 3 \times 29 = 261$
Index form: $3^2 \times 29 = 261$

Express 650 as a product of prime factors.

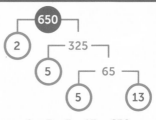

$2 \times 5 \times 5 \times 13 = 650$
Index form: $2 \times 5^2 \times 13 = 650$

Express 283 as a product of prime factors.

283 is a prime number.
Therefore, it has no prime factors.

Express 280 as a product of prime factors.

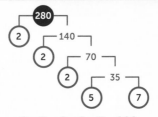

$2 \times 2 \times 2 \times 5 \times 7 = 280$
Index form: $2^3 \times 5 \times 7 = 280$

Rounding Numbers

It is not always necessary to use exact numbers, so rounding is used to provide simpler numbers that are easier to use.

Rounding Using a Number Line

Number lines are used to help determine whether to round a number up or down.

Is it nearer 600 or 700?

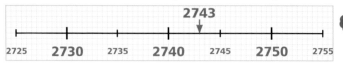

692

550   600   650   700   750   800   850

692 rounded to the nearest hundred is **700**.
The number line shows that 692 is closer to **700** than it is to **600**.

To round 2743 to the nearest ten, you need to identify whether it is nearer 2740 or 2750.

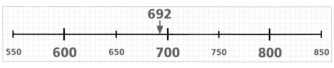

2743

2725   2730   2735   2740   2745   2750   2755

Is it nearer 2740 or 2750?

2743 rounded to the nearest ten is **2740**.
The number line shows that 2743 is closer to **2740** than it is to **2750**.

The same rule applies when rounding to decimal places.

Is it nearer 2.7 or 2.8?

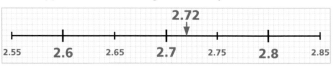

2.72

2.55   2.6   2.65   2.7   2.75   2.8   2.85

2.72 rounded to one decimal place is **2.7**.
The number line shows that 2.72 is closer to **2.7** than it is to **2.8**.
When rounding numbers to decimal places, only consider the digits **after** the decimal point.

Rounding Without a Number Line

Without a number line, look at the **first digit to the right** of the digit you are rounding.

If the number is **less than 5**, leave it alone.	**1734** rounded to the nearest hundred is **1700**. *less than 5 – leave it alone* **53.41** rounded to the nearest whole number is **53**. *less than 5 – leave it alone*

Don't forget to put in the zeros.

If the number is **5 or more**, round up.	**77** rounded to the nearest ten is **80**. *5 or more – round up* **3.14159** rounded to three decimal places is **3.142**. *5 or more – round up*

daydream
EDUCATION

Significant Figures

If something is 'significant' it is large or important.
Therefore, 'most significant' means 'largest' or 'most important'.

In the number, 169.2, the most significant figure is **1** because it has the largest value, **100**.	Hundreds	Tens	Ones		Tenths
	1	**6**	**9**	**●**	**2**

The first significant figure in a number, is the first digit that is not 0. Any leading zeros are insignificant (placeholders).	**0302.14** **00.507** **0.00621**

Rounding to Significant Figures

To round to significant figures, identify the significant figure that is being rounded to and round as normal.

To round 34562 to 1 significant figure:	**1**	Identify the first significant figure.	**34562**
	2	Look at the digit to the right of the one that is being rounding to. It is less than 5 so leave it alone.	**34562**
	3	Replace all digits after the first significant figure with zeros.	**30000**

34562 rounded to 1 significant figure is 30000.

To round 7.894 to 2 significant figures:	**1**	Identify the second significant figure.	**7.894**
	2	Look at the digit to the right of the one that is being rounding to. It is 5 or more so round up.	**7.894 → 7.9**
	3	When rounding decimals, there is no need to add zeros after the significant figures.	**7.9**

7.894 rounded to 2 significant figures is 7.9.

To round 0.0465279 to 3 significant figures:	**1**	Identify the third significant figure.	**0.0465279**
	2	Look at the digit to the right of the one that is being rounding to. It is less than 5 so leave it alone.	**0.0465279**
	3	When rounding decimals, there is no need to add zeros after the significant figures.	**0.0465**

0.0465279 rounded to 3 significant figures is 0.0465.

Decimals

Adding and Subtracting Decimals

When performing column addition or column subtraction with decimals, the decimal points and digits with the same place value must be aligned vertically. The column addition and subtraction can then be performed as normal.

Amy bought 3 t-shirts for £14.99, £23.50 and £26. How much money has Amy spent?

```
  1 4 . 9 9
  2 3 . 5 0
+ 2 6 . 0 0
-----------
  6 4 . 4 9
  1   1
```

Add zeros where necessary so the numbers with the same place value are aligned.

The three t-shirts cost £64.49

Ethan has £5.65. If he spends £2.49 on a book how much money does he have left?

```
  5 . ⁵6̸ ¹5
- 2 . 4 9
-----------
  3 . 1 6
```

Ethan is left with £3.16

Multiplying Decimals

When multiplying decimal numbers, solve the multiplication problem as normal and add in the decimal point once the calculation is complete.

To work out how many decimal digits the answer will contain, add together the number of decimal digits that there are in the question.

```
  2 . 4 6      ← 2 decimal digits
×       3
---------
  7 . 3 8      ← 2 decimal digits
  1   1
```

There are a total of **2** decimal digits in the question so there are **2** decimal digits in the answer.

```
    3 . 1 8        ← 2 decimal digits
×       6 . 8      ← 1 decimal digit
-------------
    2 5 4 4
      1 6
+ 1 9 0 8 0
    1 4
-------------
  2 1 . 6 2 4      ← 3 decimal digits
  1     1
```

There are a total of **3** decimal digits in the question (2 + 1) so there are **3** decimal digits in the answer.

daydream EDUCATION

Dividing Decimals by Whole Numbers

When dividing decimals by whole numbers, solve the division problem as normal but ensure the decimal points in the answer and the dividend are aligned vertically.

Emily, Amir, Sam and Amelia made £32.24 washing cars.

They have agreed to share the money equally between them.

How much money do they each receive?

$$4 \overline{)3\,^32\,.2\,^24} = 0\ 8.0\ 6$$

Emily, Amir, Sam and Amelia made £8.06 each.

Dividing Decimals by Decimal Numbers

When dividing a decimal number by another decimal number, follow the steps outlined below:

$$0.275 \div 0.25 \qquad\qquad 32.12 \div 0.5$$

1 Convert the **divisor** to a whole number, multiplying by the appropriate **power of 10**.

$$0.25 \times 100 = 25 \qquad\qquad 0.5 \times 10 = 5$$

2 Multiply the **dividend** by the same **power of 10**.

$$0.275 \times 100 = 27.5 \qquad\qquad 32.12 \times 10 = 321.2$$

3 Perform the division.

$$25 \overline{)2\,^27\,.5} = 0\ 1.1 \qquad\qquad 5 \overline{)3\,^32\,^21\,.2\,^20} = 0\ 6\ 4.2\ 4$$

$$0.275 \div 0.25 = 1.1 \qquad\qquad 32.12 \div 0.5 = 64.24$$

Fractions, Decimals, Percentages

Fractions, decimals and percentages are three different ways of expressing a proportion of a whole.

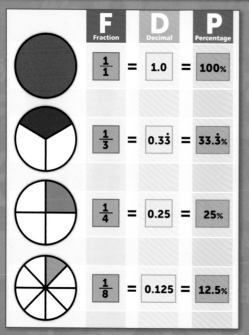

	F Fraction		**D** Decimal		**P** Percentage
	$\frac{1}{1}$	=	1.0	=	100%
	$\frac{1}{3}$	=	0.3̇3	=	33.3̇%
	$\frac{1}{4}$	=	0.25	=	25%
	$\frac{1}{8}$	=	0.125	=	12.5%

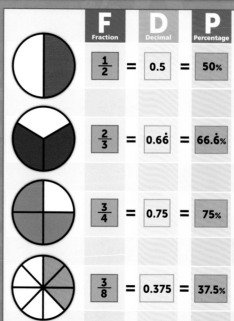

	F Fraction		**D** Decimal		**P** Percentage
	$\frac{1}{2}$	=	0.5	=	50%
	$\frac{2}{3}$	=	0.6̇6	=	66.6̇%
	$\frac{3}{4}$	=	0.75	=	75%
	$\frac{3}{8}$	=	0.375	=	37.5%

Fraction → Divide numerator by denominator → **Decimal** → Multiply by 100 → **Percentage**

$\frac{1}{5}$ → 0.20 → 20%

← Convert to a fraction* ← Divide by 100 ←

*To convert a decimal to a fraction:

1 Multiply the decimal by the appropriate power of 10 so it becomes a whole number and use this as the **numerator**.

2 The power of 10 that the decimal was multiplied by is used as the **denominator**.

3 Simplify if possible.

$0.25 \times 100 = 25$	$\frac{25}{100}$	$\frac{25}{100}$ → $\div 25$ = $\div 25$ → $\frac{1}{4}$
$0.652 \times 1000 = 652$	$\frac{652}{1000}$	$\frac{652}{1000}$ → $\div 4$ = $\div 4$ → $\frac{163}{250}$

daydream EDUCATION

Simple Fractions

When a whole or group is divided into equal parts, a fraction is created.

The top number in a fraction is called the numerator.

The bottom number in a fraction is called the denominator.

This triangle is split into three equal parts. Each part is one-third.	**This square is split into four equal parts. Each part is one-quarter.**	**This pentagon is split into five equal parts. Each part is one-fifth.**

One-third ($\frac{1}{3}$) is purple.
Two-thirds ($\frac{2}{3}$) are red.

Three-quarters ($\frac{3}{4}$) are purple.
One-quarter ($\frac{1}{4}$) is blue.

Three-fifths ($\frac{3}{5}$) are pink.
Two-fifths ($\frac{2}{5}$) are orange.

Equivalent Fractions

Equivalent fractions have different numerators and denominators but are equal in value. They are created by multiplying or dividing both numbers in the fraction by the same number.

$$\frac{1}{2} = \frac{2}{4} = \frac{4}{8}$$

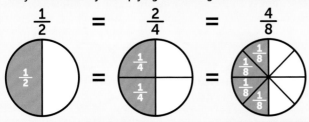

Look how these fractions take up the same amount of each circle but the numerators and denominators are different.

A fraction wall can be used to help identify equivalent fractions.

$\frac{1}{2} = \frac{4}{8}$ $\frac{1}{3} = \frac{2}{6}$

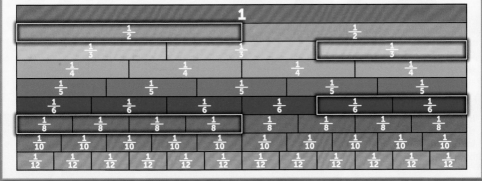

daydream EDUCATION

Simplifying & Ordering Fractions

Simplifying Fractions

To simplify a fraction the **numerator** and **denominator** must be divided by their **highest common factor** (the largest whole number that is a factor of both numbers) to create **like fractions**.

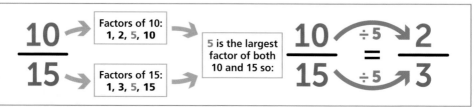

$$\frac{10}{15}$$

Factors of 10: **1, 2, 5, 10**

Factors of 15: **1, 3, 5, 15**

5 is the largest factor of both 10 and 15 so:

$$\frac{10}{15} \overset{\div 5}{\underset{\div 5}{=}} \frac{2}{3}$$

Simplifying in Steps

Sometimes it is easier to simplify in steps. Divide the top and bottom numbers of the fraction by a common factor until they cannot be divided any further.

$$\frac{60}{100} \overset{\div 10}{\underset{\div 10}{=}} \frac{6}{10} \overset{\div 2}{\underset{\div 2}{=}} \frac{3}{5}$$

Ordering Fractions

It is easy to put **like fractions** (fractions with the same **denominator**) in numerical order.

$$\frac{5}{12} \quad \frac{3}{12} \quad \frac{6}{12} \quad \frac{1}{12} \quad \Rightarrow \quad \frac{1}{12} \quad \frac{3}{12} \quad \frac{5}{12} \quad \frac{6}{12}$$

To order fractions with different **denominators**, first change all of the fractions so they have the same **denominator**.

1 Identify the lowest common multiple of the **denominators**. The lowest common multiple of **6**, **8** and **4** is **24**.

$$\frac{5}{6} \quad \frac{7}{8} \quad \frac{3}{4}$$

Multiples of 6: **6, 12, 18, 24**
Multiples of 8: **8, 16, 24, 32**
Multiples of 4: **4, 8, 12, 16, 20, 24**

2 Multiply the fractions by the appropriate numbers so that they share the same **denominator**, **24**.

$$\frac{5}{6} \overset{\times 4}{\underset{\times 4}{=}} \frac{20}{24} \qquad \frac{7}{8} \overset{\times 3}{\underset{\times 3}{=}} \frac{21}{24} \qquad \frac{3}{4} \overset{\times 6}{\underset{\times 6}{=}} \frac{18}{24}$$

3 Now that the fractions have the same **denominator**, use the **numerators** to place them in order. Then convert them back to their original form.

$$\frac{18}{24} \quad \frac{20}{24} \quad \frac{21}{24}$$

Smallest ⟶ Largest

Convert back to original form.

$$\frac{3}{4} \quad \frac{5}{6} \quad \frac{7}{8}$$

Smallest ⟶ Largest

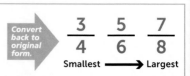

Mixed Numbers & Improper Fractions

Mixed numbers and improper fractions are two different ways of writing fractions that are greater than one, or a whole.

The fraction below can be written as a mixed number or as an improper fraction.

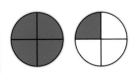

=

Mixed Numbers contain a whole number and a fractional part.

$$1\frac{1}{4}$$

=

Improper Fractions have a numerator that is greater than or equal to the denominator.

$$\frac{5}{4}$$

Converting Improper Fractions to Mixed Numbers

Divide the **numerator** by the **denominator**.

$$\frac{9}{4}$$

4 goes into 9 twice with 1 left over, therefore:

9 ÷ 4 = 2 remainder 1

You now have 2 wholes (ones) and **1** remainder, which becomes the **numerator**.

$$2\frac{1}{4}$$ ←

The **denominator** does not change.

Therefore:

$$\frac{9}{4} = 2\frac{1}{4}$$

A visual representation of the conversion is shown below.

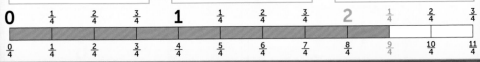

| 0 | $\frac{1}{4}$ | $\frac{2}{4}$ | $\frac{3}{4}$ | 1 | $\frac{1}{4}$ | $\frac{2}{4}$ | $\frac{3}{4}$ | 2 | $\frac{1}{4}$ | $\frac{2}{4}$ | $\frac{3}{4}$ |

| $\frac{0}{4}$ | $\frac{1}{4}$ | $\frac{2}{4}$ | $\frac{3}{4}$ | $\frac{4}{4}$ | $\frac{5}{4}$ | $\frac{6}{4}$ | $\frac{7}{4}$ | $\frac{8}{4}$ | $\frac{9}{4}$ | $\frac{10}{4}$ | $\frac{11}{4}$ |

Converting Mixed Numbers to Improper Fractions

Multiply the **denominator** by the whole number.

$$3\frac{1}{2}$$

2 × 3 = 6

Add this number to the **numerator**.

6 + 1 = 7

This creates:

$$\frac{7}{2}$$

Therefore:

$$3\frac{1}{2} = \frac{7}{2}$$

A visual representation of the conversion is shown below.

| 0 | $\frac{1}{2}$ | 1 | $\frac{1}{2}$ | 2 | $\frac{1}{2}$ | 3 | $\frac{1}{2}$ | 4 | $\frac{1}{2}$ |

| $\frac{0}{2}$ | $\frac{1}{2}$ | $\frac{2}{2}$ | $\frac{3}{2}$ | $\frac{4}{2}$ | $\frac{5}{2}$ | $\frac{6}{2}$ | $\frac{7}{2}$ | $\frac{8}{2}$ | $\frac{9}{2}$ |

27

Adding & Subtracting Fractions

To add or subtract fractions, their **denominators** must be the same.
Fractions with the same denominator are known as **like fractions**.

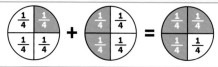

$$\frac{1}{4} + \frac{2}{4} = \frac{3}{4}$$

$$\frac{2}{3} - \frac{1}{3} = \frac{1}{3}$$

$$\frac{1}{6} + \frac{4}{6} = \frac{5}{6}$$

$$\frac{4}{5} - \frac{2}{5} = \frac{2}{5}$$

$$\frac{1}{3} + \frac{1}{3} = \frac{2}{3}$$

$$\frac{3}{4} - \frac{1}{4} = \frac{2}{4}$$

When the **denominators** are different (known as **unlike fractions**), multiply one
or both fractions, so they share the same denominator. To do this, identify the
lowest common multiple of each denominator.

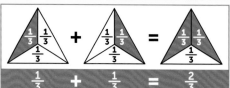

$$\frac{1}{4} + \frac{1}{3}$$

Multiples of 4	Multiples of 3
4, 8, 12, 16, 20	3, 6, 9, 12, 15

The lowest common multiple of 3 and 4 is 12.
Therefore, multiply each fraction by the
appropriate number so that they share the
lowest common denominator of 12.

$$\frac{1}{4} \overset{\times 3}{\underset{\times 3}{=}} \frac{3}{12} \qquad \frac{1}{3} \overset{\times 4}{\underset{\times 4}{=}} \frac{4}{12}$$

Add the fractions together to find the answer.
Remember to only add the **numerators**.

$$\frac{3}{12} + \frac{4}{12} = \frac{7}{12}$$

$$\frac{1}{3} - \frac{1}{6}$$

Multiples of 3	Multiples of 6
3, 6, 9	6, 12, 18

The lowest common multiple of 3 and 6 is 6.
Therefore, multiply each fraction by the
appropriate number so that they share the
lowest common denominator of 6.

$$\frac{1}{3} \overset{\times 2}{\underset{\times 2}{=}} \frac{2}{6} \qquad \frac{1}{6} \overset{\times 1}{\underset{\times 1}{=}} \frac{1}{6}$$

Perform the subtraction to find the answer.
Remember to only subtract the **numerators**.

$$\frac{2}{6} - \frac{1}{6} = \frac{1}{6}$$

daydream EDUCATION

Adding Mixed Numbers

To solve this problem, follow the steps outlined below.

$$1\tfrac{3}{4} + 2\tfrac{1}{8}$$

1 Change the mixed numbers into improper fractions.

$$1\tfrac{3}{4} \rightarrow \tfrac{4}{4} + \tfrac{3}{4} \rightarrow \tfrac{7}{4} \qquad 2\tfrac{1}{8} \rightarrow \tfrac{8}{8} + \tfrac{8}{8} + \tfrac{1}{8} \rightarrow \tfrac{17}{8}$$

$$\tfrac{7}{4} + \tfrac{17}{8}$$

2 If the denominators are different, multiply the fractions so that they share the lowest common denominator.

$$\frac{7}{4} \underset{\times 2}{\overset{\times 2}{=}} \frac{14}{8} \qquad \frac{17}{8}$$

This fraction does not need to change!

3 Add the fractions and then convert the answer back to a mixed number.

8 goes into 31 3 times with 7 remaining, **therefore:**

$$1\tfrac{3}{4} + 2\tfrac{1}{8} = 3\tfrac{7}{8}$$

$$\tfrac{14}{8} + \tfrac{17}{8} = \tfrac{31}{8}$$

$$\tfrac{31}{8} = 3\tfrac{7}{8}$$

Subtracting Mixed Numbers

To solve this problem, follow the steps outlined below.

$$2\tfrac{2}{3} - 1\tfrac{1}{2}$$

1 Change the mixed numbers into improper fractions.

$$2\tfrac{2}{3} \rightarrow \tfrac{3}{3} + \tfrac{3}{3} + \tfrac{2}{3} \rightarrow \tfrac{8}{3} \qquad 1\tfrac{1}{2} \rightarrow \tfrac{2}{2} + \tfrac{1}{2} \rightarrow \tfrac{3}{2}$$

$$\tfrac{8}{3} - \tfrac{3}{2}$$

2 If the denominators are different, multiply the fractions so that they share the lowest common denominator.

$$\frac{8}{3} \underset{\times 2}{\overset{\times 2}{=}} \frac{16}{6} \qquad \frac{3}{2} \underset{\times 3}{\overset{\times 3}{=}} \frac{9}{6}$$

3 Subtract the fraction and then convert the answer back to a mixed number.

6 goes into 7 once with 1 remaining, **therefore:**

$$2\tfrac{2}{3} - 1\tfrac{1}{2} = 1\tfrac{1}{6}$$

$$\tfrac{16}{6} - \tfrac{9}{6} = \tfrac{7}{6}$$

$$\tfrac{7}{6} = 1\tfrac{1}{6}$$

Multiplying Fractions

Simplifying Fractions

When multiplying fractions, multiply the **numerators** and the **denominators** and simplify where possible:

$$\frac{1}{2} \times \frac{3}{4} = \frac{3}{8}$$

Cannot be simplified

$$\frac{2}{5} \times \frac{3}{4} = \frac{6}{20}$$

$$\frac{6}{20} \overset{\div 2}{\underset{\div 2}{=}} \frac{3}{10}$$

$$\frac{2}{3} \times \frac{3}{4} = \frac{6}{12}$$

$$\frac{6}{12} \overset{\div 6}{\underset{\div 6}{=}} \frac{1}{2}$$

$\frac{2}{5} \times 4$

Multiplying Fractions by Whole Numbers

To solve $\frac{2}{5} \times 4$ follow the steps outlined below.

1 Write the **whole number** as a fraction. **4** becomes the **numerator** and **1** is used as the **denominator**.

$$4 \implies \frac{4}{1}$$

2 Multiply the **numerators** and then the **denominators**.

$2 \times 4 = \mathbf{8}$
$5 \times 1 = \mathbf{5}$

$$\frac{2}{5} \times \frac{4}{1} = \frac{8}{5}$$

3 Convert this answer, $\frac{8}{5}$, into a mixed number by dividing the **numerator** by the **denominator**.

$8 \div 5 = \mathbf{1}$ remainder **3**

The remainder, **3**, becomes the **numerator**, and the **denominator**, **5**, does not change.

$\frac{2}{5} \times 4 = 1\frac{3}{5}$

$8 \div 5 = 1$ remainder 3

$$\frac{8}{5} \implies 1\frac{3}{5}$$

daydream EDUCATION

$2\frac{1}{4} \times 3$

To solve $2\frac{1}{4} \times 3$ follow the steps outlined below.

1 Convert the mixed number into an improper fraction: Multiply the **denominator** by the **whole number**, and add this to the **numerator**.

$2 \times 4 = 8$; $8 + 1$ (the numerator) = **9**

This is used as the **numerator** in the improper fraction.

$$2\frac{1}{4} \Rightarrow \frac{9}{4}$$

2 Write the **whole number** as a fraction. **3** becomes the **numerator** and **1** is the **denominator**.

$$3 \Rightarrow \frac{3}{1}$$

3 Multiply the **numerators** and then the **denominators**.

$9 \times 3 = $ **27**
$4 \times 1 = $ **4**

$$\frac{9}{4} \times \frac{3}{1} = \frac{27}{4}$$

4 Convert this answer, $\frac{27}{4}$, into a mixed number by dividing the **numerator** by the **denominator**.

$27 \div 4 = $ **6** remainder 3

The remainder, **3**, becomes the **numerator**, and the **denominator** does not change.

$2\frac{1}{4} \times 3 = 6\frac{3}{4}$

$27 \div 4 = $ **6** remainder 3

$$\frac{27}{4} \Rightarrow 6\frac{3}{4}$$

 $2\frac{1}{3} \times 1\frac{4}{5}$

To solve $2\frac{1}{3} \times 1\frac{4}{5}$ follow the steps outlined below.

1 Convert the mixed numbers into improper fractions: Multiply the **denominators** by the **whole numbers** and add the answers to the **numerators**.

$2\frac{1}{3} \rightarrow 3 \times 2 = 6$; $6 + 1$ (the numerator) = 7
$1\frac{4}{5} \rightarrow 5 \times 1 = 5$; $5 + 4$ (the numerator) = 9

Use the answers as the **numerator** in the fraction.

$$2\frac{1}{3} \Rightarrow \frac{7}{3}$$
$$1\frac{4}{5} \Rightarrow \frac{9}{5}$$

2 Multiply the **numerators** and then the **denominators**.

$7 \times 9 = $ **63**
$3 \times 5 = $ **15**

$$\frac{7}{3} \times \frac{9}{5} = \frac{63}{15}$$

3 Convert the fraction into a mixed number by dividing the **numerator** by the **denominator**.

$63 \div 15 = $ **4** remainder 3

The remainder, **3**, becomes the **numerator**, and the **denominator** does not change.

$$\frac{63}{15} \Rightarrow 4\frac{3}{15}$$

$4\frac{3}{15}$ can be simplified to $4\frac{1}{5}$

Dividing Fractions

Dividing Fractions

$\frac{1}{2} \div \frac{1}{6}$ is asking how many times $\frac{1}{6}$ goes into $\frac{1}{2}$.
This can be easily identified on a fraction wall.

$\frac{1}{6}$ goes into $\frac{1}{2}$ three times.

To solve $\dfrac{4}{7} \div \dfrac{2}{3}$ follow the steps outlined below.

Step 1	Step 2	Step 3
Change the division symbol into a multiplication symbol and turn the **second fraction** upside down.	Multiply the **numerators** together followed by the **denominators**.	Simplify if possible.
$\dfrac{4}{7} \div \dfrac{2}{3} \Rightarrow \dfrac{4}{7} \times \dfrac{3}{2}$	$\dfrac{4}{7} \times \dfrac{3}{2} = \dfrac{12}{14}$	$\dfrac{12}{14} \underset{\div 2}{\overset{\div 2}{=}} \dfrac{6}{7}$

Dividing Fractions by Whole Numbers

To divide a fraction by a **whole number**, multiply the **denominator** by the **whole number** and simplify where possible.

$$\frac{1}{2} \div 4 \Rightarrow \frac{1}{2 \times 4} = \frac{1}{8}$$

If you shared $\frac{1}{2}$ a pizza between 4 people, each person would get $\frac{1}{8}$ of the whole pizza.

$\frac{1}{2}$ of a pizza $\div 4$ $= \frac{1}{8}$ each

daydream EDUCATION

Measurement

Length

The metric units of length are:
millimetres (mm), **centimetres (cm)**, **metres (m)** and **kilometres (km)**.

10 mm = 1 cm	**100 cm = 1 m**	**1,000 m = 1 km**

Although division is used to convert to a larger unit, this does not mean that 1 mm is longer than 1 cm.
1 mm is ten times shorter than 1 cm.

÷ 10 ÷ 100 ÷ 1000

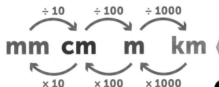

mm cm m km

× 10 × 100 × 1000

Although multiplication is used to convert to a smaller unit, this does not mean that 1 km is shorter than 1 m.
1 km is 1,000 times longer than 1 m.

Ellis jumped:
2,250 mm = 225 cm = 2.25 m

Jessica ran:
12,000 m = 12 km

Mass

The metric units of mass are:
grams (g) and **kilograms (kg)**.

1,000 g = 1 kg

÷ 1000

g kg

× 1000

750 g = 0.75 kg   **5,000 g = 5 kg**   **80,000 g = 80 kg**

Capacity

The metric units of capacity are:
millilitres (ml) and **litres (l)**.

1,000 ml = 1 l

÷ 1000

ml l

× 1000

100 ml = 0.1 l   **330 ml = 0.33 l**   **20,000 ml = 20 l**

Algebra

In algebra, letters (**variables**) can be used to represent unknown numerical values. For example, in the equation $3x + y = 16$, x and y are variables.

Key Terminology

A **term** is a collection of numbers and letters. Terms are separated by mathematical symbols.

$$3x + 4xy = 18 + y$$

An **expression** includes terms and operational (mathematical) symbols but not the equals symbol.

$$2x + 5y - 2$$

An **equation** is made up of two expressions that are equal.

$$4x + 5y = 23$$

Simplifying Algebraic Expressions

To simplify algebraic expressions, like terms can be collected together. Like terms contain the **same variable** raised to the **same power**.

Addition and Subtraction

$$a + a + a$$

can be shortened to

$$3a$$

$3a + 5a = 8a$

$4a + a = 5a$

$$4b - b$$

can be shortened to

$$3b$$

$6b - b = 5b$

$5b - 3b = 2b$

Multiplication

When multiplying (like or unlike) terms, the multiplication symbol is removed.

$a \times b$ can be shortened to ab

$3 \times a$ can be shortened to $3a$

$y \times y \times y \times y$ can be shortened to y^4 ← This is an **index** (power). It shows how many times y is multiplied by itself.

Remember $4y$ is not the same as y^4. $4y = y + y + y + y$ $y^4 = y \times y \times y \times y$

Division

$a \div b$

is written as

$$\frac{a}{b}$$

When dividing like terms, the variable can be removed from the answer.

$$\frac{15b}{3b}$$

can be shortened to

$$5$$

$$\frac{12b}{3b}$$

can be shortened to

$$4$$

daydream EDUCATION

Multiplying

When like terms with powers are **multiplied**, the powers are added.

$$y^3 \times y^4 = y^7$$
$$y \times y \times y \times y \times y \times y \times y = y^7$$
$$6^3 \times 6^4 = 6^7$$
$$6 \times 6 \times 6 \times 6 \times 6 \times 6 \times 6 = 6^7$$

Dividing

When like terms with powers are **divided**, the powers are subtracted.

$$y^5 \div y^2 = y^3$$
$$(y \times y \times y \times y \times y) \div (y \times y) = y^3$$
$$6^5 \div 6^2 = 6^3$$
$$(6 \times 6 \times 6 \times 6 \times 6) \div (6 \times 6) = 6^3$$

Important! These rules do not apply to unlike terms such as $y^2 \times x^3$ or $4^2 \times 5^3$.

Powers of Powers

When a power is **raised** to a power, multiply the powers.

$$(p^3)^2 = p^{(3 \times 2)} = p^6$$
$$(p \times p \times p) \times (p \times p \times p) = p^6$$
$$(5^3)^2 = 5^{(3 \times 2)} = 5^6$$
$$(5 \times 5 \times 5) \times (5 \times 5 \times 5) = 5^6$$

Roots

To find the **root** of a term, divide the power.

$$\sqrt{d^8} = d^{8 \div 2} = d^4$$
(check by squaring: $d^4 \times d^4 = d^8$)

$$\sqrt[3]{p^{15}} = p^{15 \div 3} = p^5$$
(check by cubing: $p^5 \times p^5 \times p^5 = p^{15}$)

Rules for Powers: One and Zero

Anything to the power of zero is one.	Anything to the power of one is itself.	One raised to any power is one.
$x^0 = 1$	$y^1 = y$	$1^n = 1$
$7^0 = 1$	$4^1 = 4$	$1^{15} = 1$

Examples

Expression	Like?	Why?	Simplified
$3b + 2b$	Yes	Same variable	$5b$
$x - y$	No	Different variables	
$x + x^4$	No	Variables raised to different powers	
$2ab + 2ba$	Yes	Same variables	$4ab$
$3x + 7y + 4x - 3y$	Yes	Same variables	$7x + 4y$
$2y + y^2 - 4$	No	Variables raised to different powers	
$2x^2 - 4x - x^2 + 2x$	Yes	Same variables and powers	$x^2 - 2x$

Solving Equations

Inverse operations are opposite operations that 'undo' each other.

Addition and Subtraction are inverse operations.

$+4$ 12 -4

$8 + 4 = 12$
$12 - 4 = 8$

8

Multiplication and Division are inverse operations.

$\times 5$ 15 $\div 5$

$3 \times 5 = 15$
$15 \div 5 = 3$

3

How to Solve Equations With Inverse Operations

The aim when solving an equation is to get the **variable** by itself on one side of the equation with a **number** on the other side – for example, $x = 2$.

When there are other operations on the same side of an equation as the variable, they need to be removed. This is done by performing the inverse (opposite) of the operation acting upon the variable. **This must be done to both sides of the equation.**

$n + 3 = 12$	$x - 7 = 1$	$5y = 20$	$\frac{m}{5} = 3$
The inverse of addition is subtraction, so subtract 3 from both sides of the equation.	The inverse of subtraction is addition, so add 7 to both sides of the equation.	The inverse of multiplication is division, so divide both sides of the equation by 5.	The inverse of division is multiplication, so multiply both sides of the equation by 5.
$n + 3 = 12$	$x - 7 = 1$	$5 \times y = 20$	$m \div 5 = 3$
$-3 \quad -3$	$+7 \quad +7$	$\div 5 \quad \div 5$	$\times 5 \quad \times 5$
$n = 9$	$x = 8$	$y = 4$	$m = 15$

The above rules do not always work for division and subtraction.
When the **variable** is the divisor, or being subtracted, solve the problem in two steps.

When the variable is being subtracted:

Add d to both sides of the equation.

Subtract 4 from both sides of the equation.

$7 - d = 4$

$+d \quad +d$

$7 = 4 + d$

$-4 \quad -4$

$3 = d$

When the variable is the divisor:

Multiply both sides of the equation by w.

Divide both sides of the equation by 3.

$\frac{12}{w} = 3$

$\times w \quad \times w$

$12 = 3w$

$\div 3 \quad \div 3$

$4 = w$

daydream EDUCATION

Max and Amy have 37 apps in total.
If Amy has 21 apps, how many does Max have?

1. Turn the question into an equation.

Use m to represent the unknown value (the number of apps Max has).	Max has __ apps Amy has 21 apps 37 apps in total
	m $+$ 21 $=$ 37

2. Solve the equation to find the value of m.

Subtraction is the inverse operation of addition so **subtract 21 from both sides of the equation.**	m $+$ 21 $=$ 37
	-21 -21
	m $=$ 16

The equation is now solved. m = 16 so Max has 16 apps.

Rohan has three pieces of wood of equal length, and one 6 cm piece. The total length of the four pieces of wood is 42 cm.

How long is each of the three equal pieces of wood?

1. Turn the question into an equation.

Use w to represent the unknown value (the length of the three equal pieces of wood).	3 pieces of wood Other piece of wood Total length
	$3 \times w$ $+$ 6 $=$ 42

2. Solve the equation to find the value of w.

Subtraction is the inverse operation of addition so **subtract 6 from both sides of the equation.**	$3w$ $+$ 6 $=$ 42
	-6 -6
Division is the inverse operation of multiplication so **divide both sides of the equation by 3.**	$3w$ $=$ 36
	$\div 3$ $\div 3$
	w $=$ 12

The equation is now solved. w = 12 so each equal piece of wood is 12 cm long.

Expanding and Factorising

Expanding Brackets

To expand brackets, multiply everything inside the brackets by the coefficient outside the brackets. This is often taught using two different methods:

The Claw Method

$$3(x + 4)$$
$$= (3 \times x) + (3 \times 4)$$
$$= 3x + 12$$

The Grid Method

$$3(x + 4)$$

×	x	$+4$
3	$3x$	12

$$= 3x + 12$$

When the term outside the brackets includes a coefficient and a variable, multiply everything inside the brackets by the coefficient and the variable.

$$2z(4x - 2y)$$
$$= (2z \times 4x) + (2z \times -2y)$$
$$= 8xz - 4yz$$

$$2z(4x - 2y)$$

×	$4x$	$-2y$
$2z$	$8xz$	$-4yz$

$$= 8xz - 4yz$$

Sometimes you will need to expand two brackets and simplify.

1. Expand each of the brackets.
2. Simplify where possible by collecting like terms.

$$4(a + 6) + 5(2a - 3)$$
$$= (4 \times a) + (4 \times 6) + (5 \times 2a) + (5 \times -3)$$
$$= 4a + 24 + 10a - 15$$
$$= 14a + 9$$

To expand double brackets, multiply every term in the first bracket by every term in the second bracket. The example below uses the grid method.

1	2	3
Draw a table with the **terms in the first bracket** written along the top and the **terms in the second bracket** written down the left hand side.	Multiply the terms across the top by the terms on the side and **write the answers in the boxes where they meet.**	Write out the terms in the table as an expression and simplify if possible.

$$(x + 2)(x - 3)$$

×	x	$+2$
x		
-3		

$$(x + 2)(x - 3)$$

×	x	$+2$
x	x^2	$2x$
-3	$-3x$	-6

$$x^2 + 2x - 3x - 6$$
$$x^2 + 2x - 3x - 6$$
$$x^2 - x - 6$$

daydream EDUCATION

Factorise - Back to Brackets

Factoring is the opposite of expanding. It involves introducing a bracket to an expression.

EXPAND

$$a(a - 3) = a^2 - 3a$$

FACTORISE

To factorise this expression, follow the steps outlined below.

$$3x - 9$$

1 Identify the Highest Common Factor (HCF) of the terms in the expression.

The HCF of $3x$ and -9 is 3.

$$3x - 9$$

Factors of $3x$:	Factors of -9:
1, 3	1, 3, 9

2 List this (3) outside the bracket.

Then divide the original terms ($3x$ and -9) by this number and place the answers within the brackets.

$$3x - 9$$
$÷3 \qquad ÷3$
$$3(x - 3)$$

3 Check your answer by expanding the bracket.

$$3(x - 3)$$
$= (3 \times x) - (3 \times -3)$
$= 3x - 9$

To factorise this expression, follow the steps outlined below.

$$12x^2 + 16xy$$

1 Identify the HCF of the terms in the expression.

The HCF of $12x^2$ and $16xy$ is $4x$.

$$12x^2 + 16xy$$

Factors of $12x^2$:	Factors of $16xy$:
$1x$, $2x$, $3x$, $4x$, $6x$...	$1x$, $2x$, $4x$, $8x$...

2 List this ($4x$) outside the bracket.

Then divide the original terms ($12x^2$ and $16xy$) by this number and place the answers within the brackets.

$$12x^2 + 16xy$$
$÷4x \qquad ÷4x$
$$4x(3x + 4y)$$

3 Check your answer by expanding the bracket.

$$4x(3x + 4y)$$
$= (4x \times 3x) + (4x \times 4y)$
$= 12x^2 + 16xy$

Substitution

When substituting in sport, one player is swapped for another. The same principle applies in algebra - a variable (letter) is swapped with a value.

What is the value of $3x + 7$ when $x = 4$?

$$3x + 7 = (3 \times x) + 7$$
$$= (3 \times 4) + 7$$
$$= 12 + 7$$
$$= 19$$

What is the value of $y^2 - 2y$ when $y = 3$?

$$y^2 - 2y = (y \times y) - (2 \times y)$$
$$= (3 \times 3) - (2 \times 3)$$
$$= 9 - 6$$
$$= 3$$

Sometimes, solving a problem involves substituting numbers into a formula.

Will gets paid **£15** an hour. If he works for 6 hours, how much does he get paid?

Total Pay = Hours × Wage

1 Substitute the known numbers into the formula.

Total Pay = 6 × £15

2 Follow the rules of **BIDMAS** to find the answer.

Total Pay = £90

Convert **86°F** from Fahrenheit to Celsius.

$$C = \frac{5(f - 32)}{9}$$

1 Substitute the known numbers into the formula.

$$C = \frac{5(86 - 32)}{9}$$

2 Follow the rules of **BIDMAS** to find the answer.

$$C = \frac{5(54)}{9} \blacktriangleright C = \frac{270}{9} \blacktriangleright C = 30$$

The cooking time for a chicken is 30 minutes per kilogram (kg), plus 40 minutes. What is the cooking time for a chicken that weighs 1.5 kg?

Cooking Time = 30 × weight + 40
$$T = 30w + 40$$

1 Substitute the known numbers into the formula.

$$T = (30 \times 1.5) + 40$$

2 Follow the rules of **BIDMAS** to find the answer.

$$T = 45 + 40$$
$$= 85$$

daydream EDUCATION

Rearranging Formulae

A **formula** is an **equation** that shows the relationship between different variables.

Sometimes you can rearrange formulae using inverse operations to make them easier to work with and solve. **In the examples below, the equations have been rearranged to make x the subject:**

$$x - 4 = 9$$
$$+4 \qquad +4$$
$$x = 13$$

◀ **Addition** and **subtraction** are inverse operations ▶

$$x + 7 = 12$$
$$-7 \qquad -7$$
$$x = 5$$

$$mx = t$$
$$\div m \qquad \div m$$
$$x = \frac{t}{m}$$

◀ **Multiplication** and **division** are inverse operations ▶

$$\frac{x}{r} = 12$$
$$\times r \qquad \times r$$
$$x = 12r$$

$$x^2 = w$$
$$\sqrt{} \qquad \sqrt{}$$
$$x = \sqrt{w}$$

◀ Finding the **square root** of a number is the inverse operation of **squaring** that number ▶

Square

$$\sqrt{x} = a$$
$$2 \qquad 2$$
$$a = x^2$$

In exams, you will often be asked to rearrange formulas so they can be solved.

You can rearrange the formula for speed to make distance or time the subject.

$$\text{Speed} = \frac{\text{Distance}}{\text{Time}}$$

OR

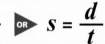

$$S = \frac{d}{t}$$

George drove for 3 hours at a speed of 32 miles per hour.
How far did he travel?

Jo ran 100 metres at a speed of 8 metres per second.
What was her time?

1 Rearrange the formula so **distance** is the subject.

$$S = \frac{d}{t}$$
$$\times t \qquad \times t$$
$$s \times t = d$$

1 Rearrange the formula so **time** is the subject.

$$S = \frac{d}{t}$$
$$\times t \qquad \times t$$
$$s \times t = d$$
$$\div s \qquad \div s$$
$$t = \frac{d}{s}$$

2 Substitute the known values into the formula and solve.

$$32 \times 3 = d$$
$$32 \times 3 = 96$$

George drove 96 miles.

2 Substitute the known values into the formula and solve.

$$t = \frac{100}{8}$$
$$t = 12.5$$

Jo's time was 12.5 seconds.

Factorising Quadratic Equations

Quadratic expressions and equations contain one or more squared terms (x^2).
The standard form of a quadratic equation is $ax^2 + bx + c = 0$.

Before solving quadratic equations always rearrange them into the form:

$$ax^2 + bx + c = 0$$

$$2n^2 = 6n - 8$$
$$-6n \qquad -6n$$
$$2n^2 - 6n = -8$$
$$+8 \qquad +8$$
$$2n^2 - 6n + 8 = 0$$

Some quadratic equations of the form $ax^2 + bx + c = 0$ (where $a \neq 1$) can be solved by factorising.

$$x^2 + 7x + 6 = 0$$

1 Find the factor pairs of c (+ 6).
1 and 6 are a factor pair of 6.
2 and 3 are a factor pair of 6.

$$1 \times 6 = 6$$
$$2 \times 3 = 6$$

2 Identify if any of the factor pairs can be added together to equal b (+ 7).

$$2 + 3 = 5 \; ✗$$
$$6 + 1 = 7 \; ✓$$

3 Split x^2 into its factors and place them inside two brackets.

$$x^2$$
$$(x \quad) \quad (x \quad)$$

4 Place each of the numbers from the factor pair into the separate brackets (including the correct symbols).

$$+6 \qquad +1$$
$$(x + 6) \quad (x + 1)$$

$x^2 + 7x + 6 = 0$ can be factorised to $(x + 6)(x + 1)$
so the solutions are: $x = 6$, $x = 1$

Remember to check your answer by expanding the brackets.

The **difference of two squares rule** is used to factorise quadratic equations in which one squared number is subtracted from another.

$$a^2 - b^2$$
$$(a - b)(a + b)$$

Look at how the following equations can be factorised using the difference of two squares rule:

$p^2 - 36$	$y^2 - 25$	$25m^2 - 9n^2$
▼	▼	▼
$(p - 6)(p + 6)$	$(y - 5)(y + 5)$	$(5m - 3n)(5m + 3n)$

daydream EDUCATION

Generating a Sequence

A sequence is a list of numbers that may be linked by a rule or pattern.

Linear Sequences

In a **linear sequence**, the difference between the terms is always the same.
The difference between each term is called the **common difference**.

Add or Subtract by the Same Amount

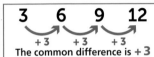

3   6   9   12
+3   +3   +3
The common difference is + 3

Rule: Add 3

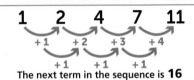

57   53   49   45
−4   −4   −4
The common difference is − 4

Rule: Subtract 4

Quadratic Sequences

In a **quadratic sequence**, the difference between the terms changes.
However, the difference between the differences is always the same.

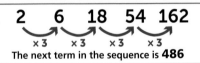

1   2   4   7   11
+1   +2   +3   +4
  +1   +1   +1
The next term in the sequence is **16**

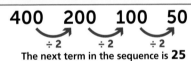

42   30   20   12   6
−12 −10 −8   −6
   −2   −2   −2
The next term in the sequence is **2**

Geometric Sequences

In a **geometric sequence**, each term is obtained by multiplying the previous term by a constant, r, called the common ratio.

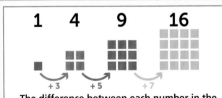

2   6   18   54   162
×3   ×3   ×3   ×3
The next term in the sequence is **486**

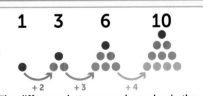

400   200   100   50
÷2   ÷2   ÷2
The next term in the sequence is **25**

Square and Triangle Numbers

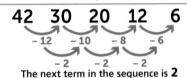

1   4   9   16
+3   +5   +7
The difference between each number in the sequence is an odd number that increases by **2**.

1   3   6   10
+2   +3   +4
The difference between each number in the sequence increases by **1**.

It is also possible to generate the next term in a picture or diagram.
Can you work out what the rules are in these picture patterns?

daydream
EDUCATION

Calculating the nth Term

When dealing with number sequences, calculating the nth term of the sequence is often necessary.

In a number sequence, **n** is used to represent the position of each item (known as a term).

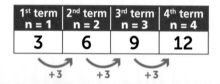

1st term n = 1	2nd term n = 2	3rd term n = 3	4th term n = 4
3	6	9	12

+3   +3   +3

The rule for this sequence is

$$+3 \times n \text{ or } +3n$$

$+3 \times 1 = \mathbf{3}$ $+3 \times 2 = \mathbf{6}$
$+3 \times 3 = \mathbf{9}$ $+3 \times 4 = \mathbf{12}$

To find the nth term rule of a linear sequence, follow the steps outlined below:

1

Calculate the **difference** between each number in the sequence.

There is a **common difference** of **+ 6** so the rule follows the 6 times table (**6n**).

n	1	2	3	4
s	4	10	16	22

The difference goes here   +6   +6   +6

6	n	

2

Compare the **common difference** to the **first number in the sequence**.

The first number in the sequence is **2 less** than the **common difference** so **– 2** is added to the rule.

The nth term rule of this sequence is 6n – 2.

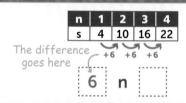

n	1	2	3	4
s	4	10	16	22

+6   +6   +6   2 less

6	n	– 2

Once you have the nth term rule, you can calculate the value of any term.

To find the 26th term in the sequence, write out the rule and then substitute 26 into the formula.

The 26th term in the sequence is 154.

$$6n - 2$$
$$(6 \times 26) - 2$$
$$156 - 2$$
$$\mathbf{154}$$

The nth term can also be calculated using the following formula:

$$dn + (a - d)$$

d = common difference   a = first term in sequence

To calculate the 12th term in this sequence, substitute the values into the formula and solve.

The 12th term is 25.

n	1	2	3	4
s	3	5	7	9

+2   +2   +2

$$dn + (a - d)$$
$$(2 \times 12) + (3 - 2)$$
$$24 + 1$$
$$\mathbf{25}$$

44

daydream
EDUCATION

Graphs and Coordinates

Coordinates are used to represent the position of a point or object on a graph.
A graph is made up of an **x-axis** and a **y-axis**.

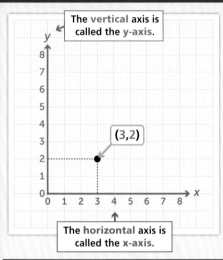

The vertical axis is called the y-axis.

The horizontal axis is called the x-axis.

The **first** number is the x-coordinate.
It gives the **horizontal** position of the point.

$$(x,y)$$

The **second** number is the y-coordinate.
It gives the **vertical** position of the point.

It is vital that the coordinates are written in the correct order. Think of the alphabet:

x before y

The coordinates of the point on the graph are (3,2).

3 → then 2 ↑

The x-axis and y-axis can be extended to create four quadrants.

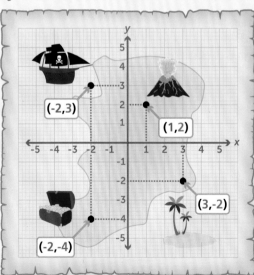

Quadrant 2

x is negative.
y is positive.

The coordinates of the ship are (-2,3).

Quadrant 3

x is negative.
y is negative.

The coordinates of the treasure are (-2,-4).

Quadrant 1

x is positive.
y is positive.

The coordinates of the volcano are (1,2).

Quadrant 4

x is positive.
y is negative.

The coordinates of the tree are (3,-2).

To help you remember the order in which coordinates are written,
remember the saying **"along the corridor and up the stairs"**.

Straight Line Graphs

Vertical and Horizontal Lines

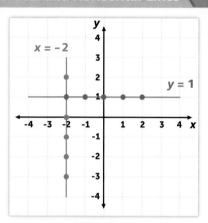

Vertical lines pass through the x-axis. All points on a vertical line have the same x-coordinate.

$x = -2$	$(-2,-2)$	$(-2,-1)$	$(-2,0)$	$(-2,1)$	$(-2,2)$

Horizontal lines pass through the y-axis. All points on a horizontal line have the same y-coordinate.

$y = 1$	$(-2,1)$	$(-1,1)$	$(0,1)$	$(1,1)$	$(2,1)$

Straight Line Equation

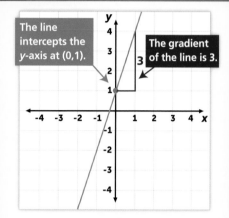

The line intercepts the y-axis at (0,1).

The gradient of the line is 3.

The standard equation of a straight line is:

$$y = mx + c$$

m = the gradient of the line.
c = the y-intercept (where the line passes through the y-axis).

The equation $y = 3x + 1$ has a:
gradient of 3
y-intercept of 1

Parallel Lines

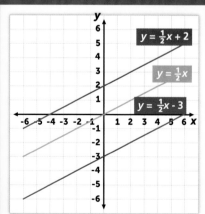

$y = \frac{1}{2}x + 2$

$y = \frac{1}{2}x$

$y = \frac{1}{2}x - 3$

Graphs that have the same gradient (value of m), are parallel and will never meet.

Graphs that pass through the origin are of the form $y = mx$. They do not contain a y-intercept (value for c), e.g. $y = \frac{1}{2}x$.

Graphs with a positive gradient slope upward from left to right, e.g. $y = 2x + 1$.

Graphs with a negative gradient slope downward from left to right, e.g. $y = -2x + 1$.

daydream EDUCATION

How to Draw Straight Line Graphs

To draw a straight line graph, you need to plot three points:
Two to draw the line and one to check the line is correct.

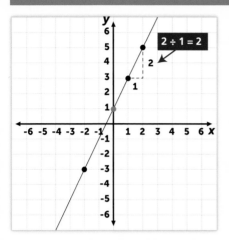

Draw the graph of $y = 2x + 1$

To identify what points to plot, work out the value of y for three different x values:

$x =$	-2	1	2
$2x$	-4	2	4
$+ 1$	-3	3	5
$y =$	-3	3	5

Plot the three points:

(-2,-3)   (1,3)   (2,5)

If the plotted points do not form a straight line, there is an error.
You can also check the **y-intercept** and the **gradient** are correct on the graph.

How to Draw Straight Line Graphs Without a Table of Values

A table of values is not always needed to plot the graph of a straight line.

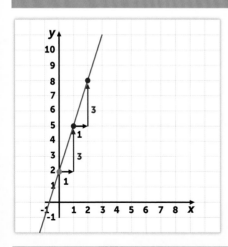

Draw the graph of $y = 3x + 2$

1 Plot the first point at the *y*-intercept. $x = 0$ and $y = 2$.

2 To plot the next point, move one unit along the *x*-axis and then move 3 (*m*) units up the *y*-axis.

3 Repeat the step above until you have plotted three points. Then connect the points to create a straight line.

If the plotted points do not form a straight line, there is an error.

Standard Graphs

Quadratic Graphs

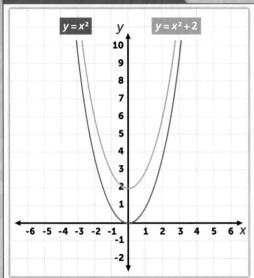

$y = x^2$ $y = x^2 + 2$

Graphs of quadratic functions contain a squared term, x^2, and are parabolas, or U-shaped.

The standard form of a quadratic function is:

$$y = ax^2 + bx + c$$

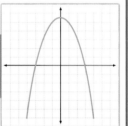

If a is negative, the parabola will be upside down.

Cubic Graphs

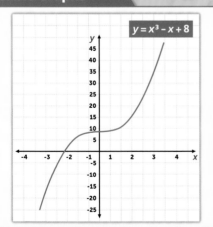

$y = x^3 - x + 8$

Graphs of a cubic function contain a cubed term, x^3. The standard form of a cubic function is:

$$y = ax^3 + bx^2 + cx + d$$

Reciprocal Graphs

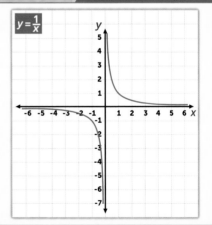

$y = \dfrac{1}{x}$

There are several forms of reciprocal functions. One of them is of the form:

$$y = \frac{k}{x}$$

where k is a real number and $x \neq 0$.

daydream
EDUCATION

Scale

Scale 1:50
0 — 50cm

The plan of Oliver's bedroom is drawn at a scale of **1:50**. This means that the bedroom is 50 times bigger in real life than in the drawing.

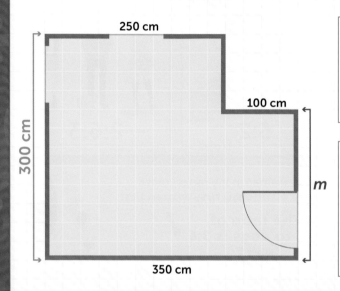

250 cm

100 cm

300 cm

m

350 cm

To identify the length of **300 cm** on the drawing, divide the real-life measurement by the scale:

300 cm ÷ 50 = **6 cm**

To identify the length of *m* in real life, use a ruler to measure the length of *m* on the drawing (in this case 4 cm) and multiply it by the scale:

4 cm × 50 = **200 cm**

Using Scales to Draw and Read Maps

The map below has a scale of **1:50,000**.
This means the map is 50,000 times smaller than the actual area shown.

Scale 1:50,000
0 — 1km

On the map the campsite is 2 cm from the church. To calculate the actual distance, multiply the measurement by the scale:

2 cm × **Scale**
2 cm × **50,000** = **100,000 cm**

Convert the measurement to the correct unit:

100,000 cm = **1 km**

Therefore, the campsite is 1 km from the church.

Ratios

A ratio is a way of comparing two or more quantities.

Purple paint is made by mixing blue and red paint in the ratio of 2 to 3.

2:3

To make mortar, sand and cement are mixed together in the ratio of 5 to 2.

5:2

Lilly, Jack and Jo have shared the money in the ratio of 2 to 6 to 3.

2:6:3

A ratio must be written in the correct order, with **the quantity mentioned first written first**.

The ratio of cats to dogs is 3:4. ✓

NOT

The ratio of dogs to cats is 3:4. ✗

Note that the ratio of dogs to cats is 4:3.

Ratios are easier to work out when they are in their simplest form.
To simplify ratios, both numbers must be **divided by their highest common factor**.

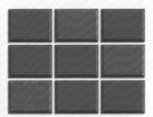

The ratio of blue to red tiles is 6 to 3 but this can be simplified.

3 is the highest common factor of 6 and 3, so divide both numbers by 3.

$$6:3$$
÷3   ÷3
$$2:1$$

Can you simplify these ratios to their simplest form?	**6:4**	**9:3**	**2:8:4**

 daydream
EDUCATION

Dividing in a Ratio

Sometimes an amount needs to be divided according to a particular ratio.

Ava, Isla and Freya made £315 selling balloons at a fayre. They agreed to split the money in the ratio of 3:2:4. How much money does each person get?

1	Add the numbers in the ratio to calculate the total number of parts.	$3 + 2 + 4 = 9$
2	Find the value of 1 part by dividing the total amount by the total number of parts, 9.	$315 \div 9 = 35$ **1 part = 35**
3	Multiply the value of 1 part, **35**, by the numbers in the ratio to calculate how much money each person gets.	$3 \times 35 = 105$ $2 \times 35 = 70$ $4 \times 35 = 140$
4	**315** divided in the ratio of **3:2:4** is **105:70:140**. Check your answer by adding together the values.	Ava Isla Freya £105 £70 £140 $105 + 70 + 140 = 315$

If you know the value of one part of a ratio, you can calculate the values of the other parts, and the total sum of the ratio.

To make turquoise paint, blue paint and green paint are mixed in the ratio of **4:7**. If Eva has **2.4 litres of blue paint**, how much green paint does she need and how much turquoise paint can she make?

1	Calculate the value of 1 part by dividing the amount of blue paint by the number of blue parts in the ratio.	$2.4 \div 4 = 0.6$ **1 part** = 0.6
2	To calculate the amount of green paint that is needed, multiply the value of 1 part by the number of green parts in the ratio.	$0.6 \times 7 = 4.2$ Eva needs 4.2 litres of green paint.
3	To calculate the amount of turquoise paint that Eva can make, multiply the value of 1 part by the total number of parts in the ratio.	$0.6 \times 11 = 6.6$ Eva can make 6.6 litres of turquoise paint.

Direct Proportion

Two quantities are in **direct proportion** if they increase or decrease in the same ratio, or at the same rate.

If y is directly proportional to x, then $y \propto x$

When two variables are **directly proportional** they form a **straight line graph** that passes through the origin.

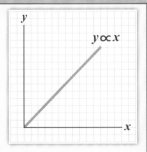

In the examples below the value of one variable is directly proportional to the other.

Number of drinks ∝ Cost of drink	Value of pound ∝ Value of dollar
1 drink : £1.20	£1 : $1.50
3 drinks : £3.60	£25 : $37.50
152 drinks : £182.40	£420 : $630

Direct Proportion Problems

Mason is making 30 biscuits. He needs: 300g of flour, 250g of butter, 140g of sugar and 2 eggs. How much flour will he need for 45 biscuits?

Step 1 - Calculate how much flour is needed to make 1 biscuit.

$$\text{Flour in 1 biscuit} = \frac{\text{total amount of flour}}{\text{number of biscuits}} = \frac{300}{30} = 10$$

Step 2 - Calculate how much flour is needed for 45 biscuits.

$$10 \times 45 = 450$$

Mason will need 450g of flour to make 45 biscuits.

If 3 books cost £9.90, how much do 5 books cost?

Step 1 - Calculate the cost of 1 book.

$$\text{Cost of 1 book} = \frac{\text{total cost of books}}{\text{original number of books}} = \frac{9.9}{3} = 3.30$$

Step 2 - Calculate the cost of 5 books.

$$3.30 \times 5 = 16.50$$

The cost of 5 books would be £16.50.

daydream EDUCATION

Inverse Proportion

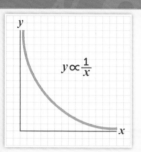

$y \propto \frac{1}{x}$

Two variables are **inversely proportional** if the value of one increases at the same rate as the other decreases.

If y is inversely proportional to x, then $y \propto \frac{1}{x}$

When two variables are **inversely proportional** they form a **curved graph** that slopes down from left to right.

A simple example of inverse proportion is shown below.

If you double the length of a rectangle, you have to reduce the width by half to keep the area of the rectangle the same.

The length and width of the rectangles are inversely proportional.

3 m

6 m² 2 m

6 m

6 m² 1 m

Inverse Proportion Problems

Chloe is filling up a swimming pool. If she uses 4 pipes, it takes 60 minutes. How long will it take her if she uses 6 pipes?

Step 1

Multiply the time taken by the original number of pipes.

$60 \times 4 = 240$

Step 2

Divide the answer by the new number of pipes.

$240 \div 6 = 40$

It would take Chloe 40 minutes to fill up the pool with 6 pipes.

It takes 2 people 90 minutes to paint a fence. How long will it take 5 people?

Step 1

Multiply the time taken by the original number of people.

$90 \times 2 = 180$

Step 2

Divide the answer by the new number of people.

$180 \div 5 = 36$

It would take 5 people 36 minutes to paint a fence.

Percentages

1%

20%

50%

100%

Percentages and Fractions

To convert from a percentage to a fraction:

1. Make the percentage the numerator of the fraction.

$$30\% = \frac{30}{}$$

2. *Per cent* means 'out of every 100' so 100 is used as the denominator.

$$\frac{30}{100}$$

3. Simplify if possible.

$$\frac{30}{100} \rightarrow \frac{\div 10}{\div 10} \rightarrow = \frac{3}{10}$$

To convert from a fraction to a percentage:

1. Divide the numerator by the denominator.

$$\frac{30}{100} = 0.3$$

2. Multiply by 100.

$$0.3 \times 100 = 30$$

3. Add a percent symbol.

$$30\%$$

Percentages and Decimals

To convert a percentage to a decimal, remove the percent symbol and divide by 100.

$\div 100$

$$25\% = 0.25$$

$\times 100$

To convert a decimal to a percentage, multiply the decimal by 100 and add a percent symbol.

daydream EDUCATION

What is 20% of 40?

Method 1 - Convert to a Decimal

1. Convert the percentage into a decimal.

$$20 \div 100 = 0.2$$

2. Multiply the amount by the decimal.

$$40 \times 0.2 = 8$$

20% of 40 is 8

Method 2 - Finding 10%

1. Find 10% by dividing the amount by 10.

$$40 \div 10 = 4$$

2. Multiply the answer by 2 to get 20%.

$$4 \times 2 = 8$$

20% of 40 is 8

For more complex calculations you can use the finding 1% method.

What is 24% of 250?

1. Find 1% by dividing the amount by 100.

$$250 \div 100 = 2.5$$

2. Multiply the answer by 24 to get 24%.

$$2.5 \times 24 = 60$$

24% of 250 is 60

Expressing One Quantity as a Percentage of Another

Percentages are used to express how large or small one amount is relative to another amount. For example, percentages are often used to express exam results.

Harry scored 30 out of 50 in his maths exam. What is his score as a percentage?

1. Divide Harry's score by the total number of questions.

$$\frac{30}{50} = 0.6$$

2. Multiply the answer by 100.

$$0.6 \times 100 = 60$$

Harry scored **60%** in his maths exam.

Evie is practicing her penalties. She scores 24 out of 30. What is her success rate as a percentage?

1. Divide Evie's score by the total number of penalties.

$$\frac{24}{30} = 0.8$$

2. Multiply the answer by 100.

$$0.8 \times 100 = 80$$

Evie scored **80%** of her penalties.

Percentage Change

Percentage Increase

To calculate a percentage increase, find the value of the percentage and **add** it to the original amount.

Charlie's car cost £250 + VAT (20%) to get repaired. What was the cost including VAT?

1 | Calculate 20%:
20% of 250 = 50

2 | Add it to the original amount:
250 + 50 = 300

The total cost of the repairs was
£300

Percentage Decrease

To calculate a percentage decrease, find the value of the percentage and subtract it from the original amount.

A dress costs £40 but there is a 10% sale on. What does the dress cost in the sale?

1 | Calculate 10%:
10% of 40 = 4

2 | Subtract it from the original amount:
40 – 4 = 36

The sale price of the dress is
£36

Percentage Change

$$\text{Percentage change} = \frac{\text{Change in value}}{\text{Original value}} \times 100$$

Last year Sienna had £3,200 in her bank account. She now has £3,360 despite not paying in any money.

Calculate the rate of interest on her account.

1 | Calculate the change in value (balance):
3360 – 3200 = 160

2 | Divide the change in balance by the original balance:
160 ÷ 3200 = 0.05

3 | Multiply by 100:
0.05 × 100 = 5

The rate of interest on Sienna's account was
5%

daydream
EDUCATION

Angles and Their Measurement

The turn, or rotation, between two meeting lines is called an angle.
Angles are measured in degrees (°), often with a protractor or angle measurer.

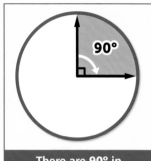

There are **90°** in
one-quarter of a rotation.

There are **180°**
in half a rotation.

There are **360°**
in one complete rotation.

Acute Angles

Angles less than 90° are called
acute angles.

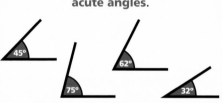

Right Angles

Angles that are 90° are **right angles**
and are marked with a small square.

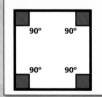 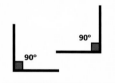

Obtuse Angles

Angles greater than 90° but less than
180° are called **obtuse angles**.

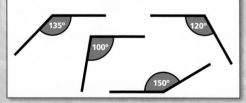

Reflex Angles

Angles greater than 180°
are called **reflex angles**.

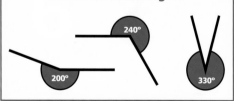

Can you estimate and measure
the size of these angles here?
Are they **acute**, **obtuse**,
right or **reflex** angles?

daydream EDUCATION

Angle Properties

Take a triangle

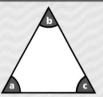

Angles add up to 180°

Tear off the angles

They add up to 180°

Angles on a straight line add up to 180°

Take a quadrilateral

Angles add up to 360°

Tear off the angles

They add up to 360°

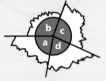

Angles around a point add up to 360°

The sum of the interior angles of a polygon can be calculated using the formula:

(n - 2) x 180

where n = number of sides

Angle Properties of Parallel Lines

Corresponding Angles

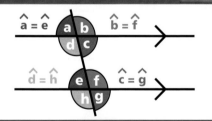

$\hat{a} = \hat{e}$ $\hat{b} = \hat{f}$

$\hat{d} = \hat{h}$ $\hat{c} = \hat{g}$

Vertically Opposite Angles

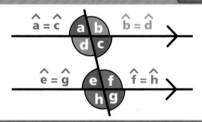

$\hat{a} = \hat{c}$ $\hat{b} = \hat{d}$

$\hat{e} = \hat{g}$ $\hat{f} = \hat{h}$

Alternate Angles

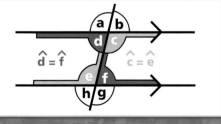

$\hat{d} = \hat{f}$ $\hat{c} = \hat{e}$

Interior Angles

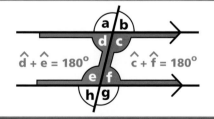

$\hat{d} + \hat{e} = 180°$ $\hat{c} + \hat{f} = 180°$

daydream
EDUCATION

Quadrilaterals

Quadrilaterals have 4 sides and 4 angles. The interior angles always add up to 360°.

Square

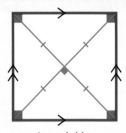

4 equal sides
4 right angles (90°)
Opposite sides are parallel
Diagonals are equal and bisect each other at 90°

Rectangle

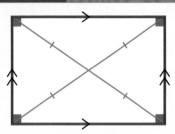

Opposite sides are equal
4 right angles (90°)
Opposite sides are parallel
Diagonals are equal and bisect each other

Rhombus

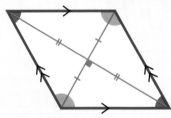

4 equal sides
Opposite angles are equal
Opposite sides are parallel
Diagonals are not equal (unless the rhombus is a square) but bisect each other at 90°

Parallelogram

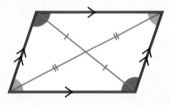

Opposite sides are equal
Opposite angles are equal
Opposite sides are parallel
Diagonals are not equal (unless the parallelogram is a rectangle) but bisect each other

Trapezium

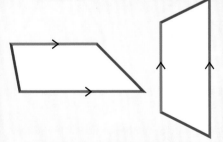

4 sides of varying lengths
One pair of opposite sides are parallel

Kite

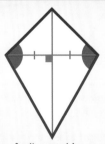

2 pairs of adjacent sides are equal
1 diagonal bisects the other at 90°
1 pair of opposite angles is equal

Polygons

Polygons are 2D shapes that have three sides or more, are made of straight lines and are closed (no open sides).

Regular Polygons

A polygon is regular if all of its sides and interior angles are equal.

Triangle

3 sides, 3 equal angles

Quadrilateral

4 sides, 4 equal angles

Pentagon

5 sides, 5 equal angles

Octagon

8 sides, 8 equal angles

Irregular Polygons

An irregular polygon can have sides of any length and interior angles of any size.

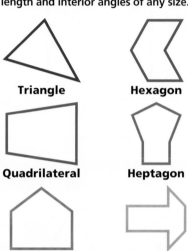

Triangle

Hexagon

Quadrilateral

Heptagon

Pentagon

Octagon

Sum of Interior Angles

Any polygon can be broken down into a number of triangles. Dividing a polygon up in this way can help you calculate the sum of it's internal angles.

The internal angles of a triangle add up to **180°**. Therefore, the sum of the internal angles of a polygon can be calculated by splitting it up into triangles and multiplying the number of triangles by 180.

Triangle

180°

3 sides, 1 triangle
$1 \times 180° = 180°$

Quadrilateral

180°

180°

4 sides, 2 triangles
$2 \times 180° = 360°$

Pentagon

180° 180°

180°

5 sides, 3 triangles
$3 \times 180° = 540°$

Hexagon

180°

180°

180°

180°

6 sides, 4 triangles
$4 \times 180° = 720°$

The number of triangles in a polygon is always 2 less than its number of sides. Therefore, the following formula can be used to calculate the sum of interior angles of a polygon:

Sum of interior angles = 180(n-2) where **n** = number of sides

daydream
EDUCATION

Types of Triangles

Equilateral

(Equi = Equal, *Lateral* = Sides)

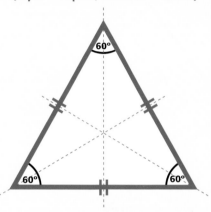

3 equal sides
3 equal interior angles (each 60°)
3 lines of symmetry

Isosceles

(Greek for 'two equal sides')

2 equal sides
2 equal interior angles (base angles)
1 line of symmetry

Right Angle

(Right angle = 90°)

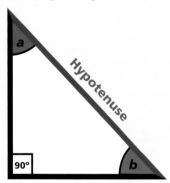

One interior angle is a right angle (90°)
The two other angles add up to 90° (*a* + *b* = 90°)
There is no symmetry unless angles *a* and *b* are 45°
The longest side is called the hypotenuse

Scalene

(*Skalēnos*, unequal in Greek)

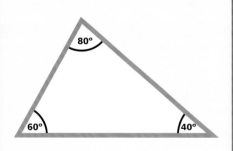

All interior angles are different
All sides are different
There are no lines of symmetry

Remember: The interior angles of a triangle always add up to 180°.

Pythagoras' Theorem

The square of the hypotenuse (the longest side, opposite the right angle), is equal to the sum of the squares of the other two sides.

Pythagoras discovered that when you draw a square onto each side of a right-angled triangle, the area of the two smaller squares added together, equals the area of the largest square.

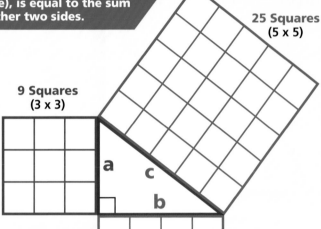

25 Squares (5 x 5)

9 Squares (3 x 3)

16 Squares (4 x 4)

a c b

$$a^2 + b^2 = c^2$$
$$3^2 + 4^2 = 5^2$$
$$9 + 16 = 25$$

When you know the lengths of any two sides, you can find the length of the third side.

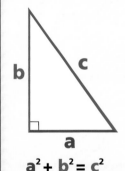

therefore...

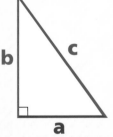

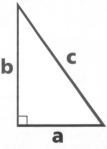

$a^2 + b^2 = c^2$	$a^2 = c^2 - b^2$	$b^2 = c^2 - a^2$

REMEMBER: Pythagoras' theorem only applies to right-angled triangles.

daydream EDUCATION

Trigonometry

Trigonometry deals with the relationship between the sides and angles of a triangle. In right-angled triangles, the following rules apply.

For the angle θ, the sides of the triangle are labelled as shown:

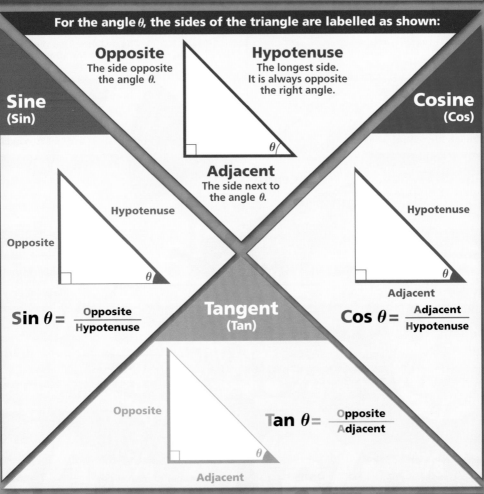

Opposite
The side opposite the angle θ.

Hypotenuse
The longest side. It is always opposite the right angle.

Adjacent
The side next to the angle θ.

Sine (Sin)

$$Sin\ \theta = \frac{Opposite}{Hypotenuse}$$

Cosine (Cos)

$$Cos\ \theta = \frac{Adjacent}{Hypotenuse}$$

Tangent (Tan)

$$Tan\ \theta = \frac{Opposite}{Adjacent}$$

An easy way to remember these rules is to use the phrase:

SOH - CAH - TOA

$$Sin\ \theta = \frac{Opposite}{Hypotenuse}$$

$$Cos\ \theta = \frac{Adjacent}{Hypotenuse}$$

$$Tan\ \theta = \frac{Opposite}{Adjacent}$$

The values of $\sin\theta$, $\cos\theta$ and $\tan\theta$ for 0°, 30°, 45°, 60° and 90° are shown below.

0°	30°	45°	60°	90°
0	$\frac{1}{2}$	$\frac{1}{\sqrt{2}}$	$\frac{\sqrt{3}}{2}$	1

0°	30°	45°	60°	90°
1	$\frac{\sqrt{3}}{2}$	$\frac{1}{\sqrt{2}}$	$\frac{1}{2}$	0

0°	30°	45°	60°	90°
0	$\frac{1}{\sqrt{3}}$	1	$\sqrt{3}$	n/a

daydream EDUCATION

Circle Properties

Circumference
The outer edge of a circle

Radius
The distance from the centre to the edge; half the diameter (plural radii.)

Diameter
The distance from edge to edge passing through the centre

Sector
The area enclosed by an arc and two radii

Chord
A straight line joining any two points on the circumference

Arc
A part of the circumference

Segment
The area inside a circle enclosed by an arc and a chord

Tangent
A straight line that touches a circle at one point only

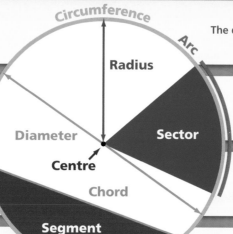

There is a constant relationship between the circumference and diameter of any circle. This is denoted by the greek letter π (pi):

$$\pi = \frac{\text{Circumference}}{\text{Diameter}} = 3.14$$

π is an irrational number. Its decimal representation never ends or repeats: 3.141592653589...

Circumference
The circumference of a circle can be calculated using the diameter or the radius:

Circumference = π × Diameter (C = π d)

or

Circumference = 2 × π × Radius (C = 2 π r)

Diameter
The diameter of a circle can be calculated using the circumference.

$$\text{Diameter} = \frac{\text{Circumference}}{\pi} \quad \left(d = \frac{C}{\pi} \right)$$

Area
The area of a circle can be calculated using the radius:

Area = π × Radius × Radius (A = π r^2)

daydream EDUCATION

Circle Theorems

Angles in the same segment and standing on the same chord are always equal.

The angle at the centre of a circle is twice the angle at the circumference (outer edge).

The angle in a semi-circle is always 90°.

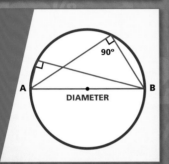

ABCD is a **cyclic quadrilateral** - all vertices lie on the circumference of the circle. Diagonally opposite angles add up to 180°.

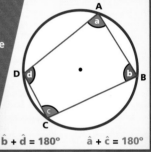

$\hat{b} + \hat{d} = 180°$ $\qquad$ $\hat{a} + \hat{c} = 180°$

A line drawn from the centre of a circle to the mid-point of a chord is perpendicular (at 90°) to the chord.

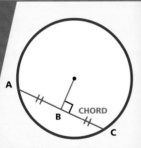

The angle between the tangent and the radius is always 90°.

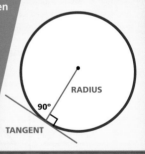

Tangents from a common point (A) to a circle are always equal in length.

AB = AC

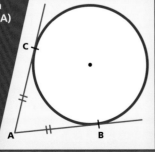

The angle between the tangent and the side of the triangle is equal to the interior opposite angle.

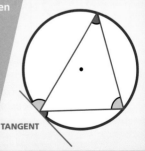

Transformations

A translation moves every point on a shape the same distance in the same direction.

Shape **A** has been translated +3 units along the x-axis and +2 units up the y-axis.

Shape **C** has been translated -6 units along the x-axis and +3 units up the y-axis.

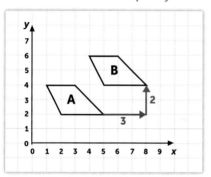

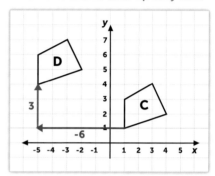

The translation **A** to **B** expressed as a vector is $\begin{bmatrix} 3 \\ 2 \end{bmatrix}$.

The translation **C** to **D** expressed as a vector is $\begin{bmatrix} -6 \\ 3 \end{bmatrix}$.

In a translation, the shapes are congruent. This means that one shape can be turned, flipped or moved so it fits exactly on the other.

Reflection

A reflection produces a mirror image of a shape along a line of reflection.

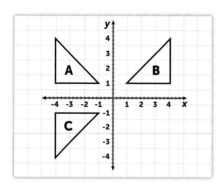

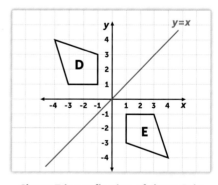

B is a reflection of **A** across the y-axis.
C is a reflection of **A** across the x-axis.

Shape **E** is a reflection of shape **D** in the line y=x.

In a reflection, the shapes are congruent. This means that one shape can be turned, flipped or moved so it fits exactly on the other.

daydream EDUCATION

Rotation

A rotation turns a shape about a fixed point.
To perform a rotation, three details are needed:

1 The centre of rotation **2** The angle of rotation **3** The direction of rotation

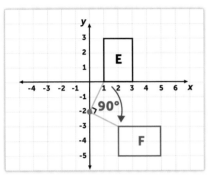

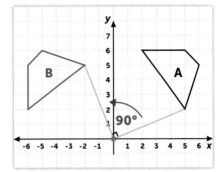

Shape **F** is a rotation of shape **E** 90°
clockwise about (0,-2).

Shape **B** is a rotation of shape **A** 90°
anticlockwise about the origin (0,0).

In a rotation, the shapes are congruent. This means that one shape can be turned, flipped or moved so it fits exactly on the other.

Enlargement

To perform an enlargement, two pieces of information are needed:

1 The centre of enlargement – the point from which the object is enlarged **2** The scale factor – the size of the enlargement

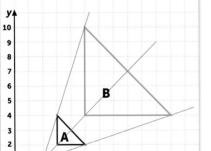

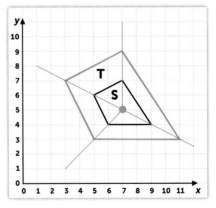

Shape **B** is an enlargement of shape **A**
by a scale factor of 3, centre (2,1).

Shape **T** is an enlargement of shape **S**
by a scale factor of 2, centre (7,5).

In an enlargement, the shapes are similar. The shapes are not the same size but their angles are the same size and their lengths are proportionate to each other.

Three-Figure Bearings

A bearing is the direction of travel measured clockwise from the north line. All bearings are written using three figures (e.g. 050° rather than 50°).

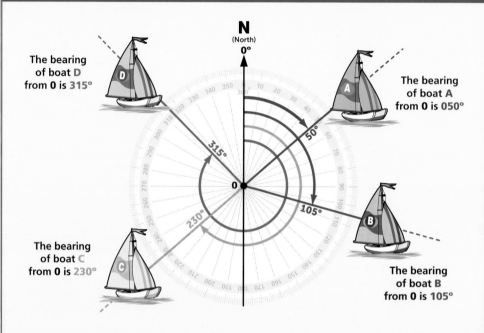

The bearing of boat D from 0 is 315°

The bearing of boat A from 0 is 050°

The bearing of boat C from 0 is 230°

The bearing of boat B from 0 is 105°

To find the bearing of the boat from the lifeguard station, follow the steps outlined below.

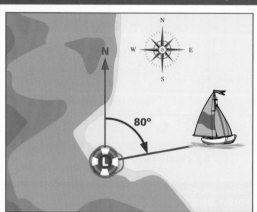

Step 1: Draw the north line at the lifeguard station (L).

Step 2: Draw a line from the lifeguard station to the boat.

Step 3: Measure the angle clockwise from the north line.

The size of the angle is **80°**. Therefore, the three-figure bearing of the boat from the lifeguard station is **080°**.

daydream EDUCATION

Solids and Their Nets

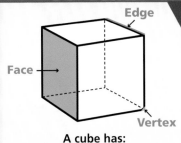

Edge

Face →

Vertex

A solid figure has **faces**, **edges** and **vertices** (corners). A net is the surface of a solid shape folded out flat.

A net can often be configured in several ways.

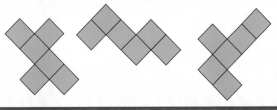

A cube has:
6 faces, 12 edges, 8 vertices

Cuboid

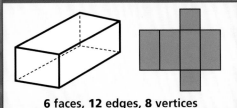

6 faces, **12** edges, **8** vertices

Triangular Prism

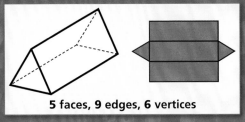

5 faces, **9** edges, **6** vertices

Cylinder

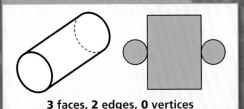

3 faces, **2** edges, **0** vertices

Cone

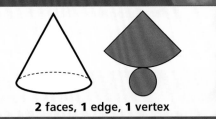

2 faces, **1** edge, **1** vertex

Square-based Pyramid

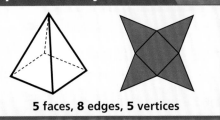

5 faces, **8** edges, **5** vertices

Triangular-based Pyramid

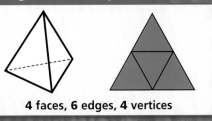

4 faces, **6** edges, **4** vertices

The surface area of a solid figure is equal to the total area of its net. To work out the surface area of a shape add together the areas of the separate faces of the net.

Area

Area is the total size of a flat surface. It is the amount of space inside the perimeter.

Rectangle/Square

What is the area of the football field?

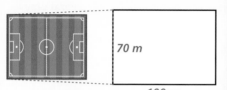

70 m

100 m

Area of rectangle = *length × width*
= *100 × 70*
Area of field = **7,000 m²**

Triangle

What is the area of the sign?

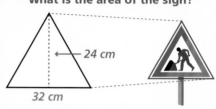

← 24 cm

32 cm

Area of triangle = $\frac{1}{2}$ × *base × height*
= $\frac{1}{2}$ × *32 × 24*
Area of sign = **384 cm²**

Parallelogram

What is the area of the side face of the rubber?

7 mm

38 mm

Area of parallelogram = *base × height*
= *38 × 7*
Area of side face = **266 mm²**

Trapezium

What is the area of the roof?

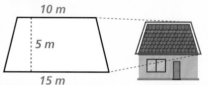

10 m

5 m

15 m

Area of trapezium = $\frac{1}{2}$ × *(a + b) × height*
= $\frac{1}{2}$ × *(10 + 15) × 5*
= $\frac{1}{2}$ × *(25) × 5*
Area of roof = **62.5 m²**

Compound Shapes

When measuring the area of a compound shape, break it down into simpler shapes and then add the areas together. Look at the plan of the room below.

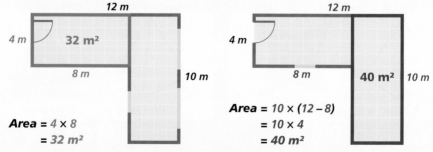

12 m

4 m   **32 m²**

8 m

10 m

Area = *4 × 8*
= *32 m²*

12 m

4 m

8 m

40 m²   10 m

Area = *10 × (12 − 8)*
= *10 × 4*
= *40 m²*

Total area of the compound shape: 32 m² + 40 m² = 72 m²

daydream
EDUCATION

Volume

Volume is the amount of space inside a 3D shape or object.

Prisms and Cylinders

Solid objects that maintain a constant cross-sectional area along their length.

Volume of prism/cylinder = *cross-sectional area* × *length*

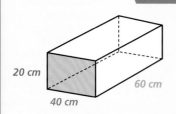

$V = w \times h \times l$
$= 40 \times 20 \times 60$
$= 48,000 \text{ cm}^3$

20 cm, 40 cm, 60 cm

$V = \frac{1}{2} \times b \times h \times l$
$= \frac{1}{2} \times 2 \times 1.5 \times 3.5$
$= 5.25 \text{ m}^3$

1.5 m, 3.5 m, 2 m

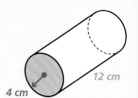

$V = \pi r^2 \times l$
$= \pi \times 16 \times 12$
$= 603.19 \text{ cm}^3 \text{ (2 d.p)}$

4 cm, 12 cm

Pyramids and Cones

3D shapes that narrow to a common vertex, creating a point.

Volume of pyramid/cone = $\frac{1}{3}$ *area of base* × *height*

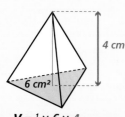

$V = \frac{1}{3} \times 6 \times 4$
$= 8 \text{ cm}^3$

4 cm, 6 cm²

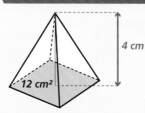

$V = \frac{1}{3} \times 12 \times 4$
$= 16 \text{ cm}^3$

4 cm, 12 cm²

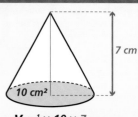

$V = \frac{1}{3} \times 10 \times 7$
$= 23.3 \text{ cm}^3 \text{ (1 d.p.)}$

7 cm, 10 cm²

Spheres

A perfectly round 3D shape. Every point on its surface is equidistant from its centre.

Volume of sphere = $\frac{4}{3} \pi r^3$

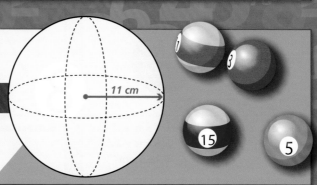

11 cm

$V = \frac{4}{3} \pi r^3$
$= \frac{4}{3} \times \pi \times 11^3$
$= \frac{4}{3} \times \pi \times 1,331$
$= 5575.28 \text{ cm}^3 \text{ (2 d.p.)}$

Surface Area

Surface area is the total area of the outer surface of a 3D object. The surface area of a solid figure is equal to the total area of its net. To calculate the surface area of a shape, work out the area of each face and add them together.

Triangular Prism

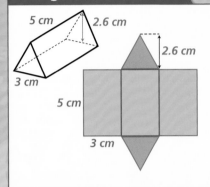

1 Calculate the areas of the different sized faces:

Area = $l \times w$	Area = $\frac{1}{2} \times b \times h$
= 5 × 3	= $\frac{1}{2}$ × 3 × 2.6
= 15 cm²	= 3.9 cm²

2 Multiply these areas by the number of corresponding faces:

15 × 3 = 45 cm²   3.9 × 2 = 7.8 cm²

3 Add the areas together: 45 + 7.8 = 52.8 cm².

Square-based Pyramid

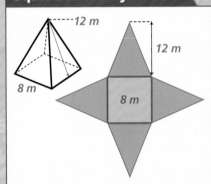

1 Calculate the areas of the different sized faces:

Area = $l \times w$	Area = $\frac{1}{2} \times b \times h$
= 8 × 8	= $\frac{1}{2}$ × 8 × 12
= 64 m²	= 48 m²

2 Multiply the area of the triangular face by the number of corresponding faces:

48 × 4 = 192 m²

3 Add the areas together: 192 + 64 = 256 m².

Sphere

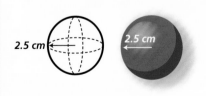

Surface area of sphere = 4 × π × r^2
= 4 × π × 2.5^2
= 78.5 cm²

Cone

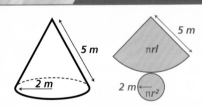

πrl

πr^2

Surface area of cone = π × r × l + π × r^2
= π × 2 × 5 + π × 2^2
= 31.41 + 12.57
= 43.98 m²

daydream
EDUCATI

Averages

An average is a measure of the middle value of a data set. There are three main types of averages: mean, mode and median.

1 Mean

The mean is the sum of the values divided by the number of values.

$$\text{Mean} = \frac{\text{Sum of values}}{\text{Number of values}}$$

Joe was pleased with his exam results:

Geography	Biology	French	English	Maths	Music	Art
88%	72%	79%	77%	81%	68%	88%

His mean mark was $= \dfrac{88 + 72 + 79 + 77 + 81 + 68 + 88}{7} = \dfrac{553}{7} = \mathbf{79\%}$

2 Mode

Geography	Art
88%	88%

The mode is the value that occurs most often.

The mode for Joe's results was 88%. It occurred twice, in Geography and Art.

3 Median

The median is the middle value when the data is arranged in order of size.

Music	Biology	English	French	Maths	Geography	Art
68%	72%	77%	79%	81%	88%	88%

The median for Joe's results is 79% because the French result is in the middle.
If there is an even number of values, then the median is the mean of the middle two values.

Range

The range is the difference between the lowest value and the highest value in a data set.

Music	Biology	English	French	Maths	Geography	Art
68%	72%	77%	79%	81%	88%	88%

Range = 20

To find the range, subtract the lowest value from the highest value. The range of Joe's results is 20.

Probability

Probability is used in everyday life to predict the chances of things happening.

Probability is Measured on a Scale of 0 - 1

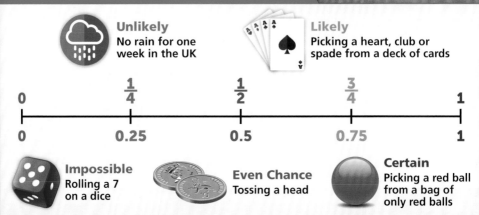

Unlikely
No rain for one week in the UK

Likely
Picking a heart, club or spade from a deck of cards

0	$\frac{1}{4}$	$\frac{1}{2}$	$\frac{3}{4}$	1
0	0.25	0.5	0.75	1

Impossible
Rolling a 7 on a dice

Even Chance
Tossing a head

Certain
Picking a red ball from a bag of only red balls

Estimated Probability = $\frac{\text{Number of Successful Events}}{\text{Total Number of Events}}$

The probability of scoring a 4 when rolling a dice is $\frac{1}{6}$

$$P(4) = \frac{1}{6}$$

The probability of picking a club from a deck of cards is $\frac{1}{4}$

$$P(Club) = \frac{13}{52} \text{ or } \frac{1}{4}$$

Listing All Outcomes

Listing all possible outcomes of an event can help when calculating probabilities, making it less likely that outcomes are missed.

The table below lists all 20 possible outcomes of the two spinners.

	Red (R)	Green (G)	Orange (O)	Green (G)
1	1R	1G	1O	1G
2	2R	2G	2O	2G
3	3R	3G	3O	3G
5	5R	5G	5O	5G
1	1R	1G	1O	1G

The probability of spinning a 2 and a red (2R) is: $\frac{1}{20}$

The probability of spinning a 1 and a green (1G) is: $\frac{4}{20}$ or $\frac{1}{5}$

daydream EDUCATIO

Independent and Dependent Events

The probability of picking a heart from a deck of cards is: **25%** $\frac{13}{52}$ or $\frac{1}{4}$ **0.25**

Independent Events

Events are **independent** if the outcome of one **does not** affect the outcome of another.

If the card is replaced, the probability of picking a heart the next time remains the same, $\frac{13}{52}$ or $\frac{1}{4}$.

The outcome of the two events can be calculated by multiplying the probabilities:

P(heart,heart) = $\frac{1}{4} \times \frac{1}{4} = \frac{1}{16}$

Dependent Events

Events are **dependent** if the outcome of one affects the outcome of another.

If the card is not replaced, the probability of picking a heart the next time changes to $\frac{12}{51}$ or $\frac{4}{17}$.

The outcome of the two events can be calculated by multiplying the probabilities:

P(heart,heart) = $\frac{1}{4} \times \frac{4}{17} = \frac{4}{68}$ or $\frac{1}{17}$

Probability Tree Diagrams

Tree diagrams display all the possible outcomes of a series of events and help solve probability problems. Each branch in a tree diagram represents an outcome.

First Toss	Second Toss	Outcome		Probability

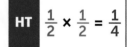
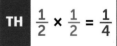

HH $\frac{1}{2} \times \frac{1}{2} = \frac{1}{4}$

HT $\frac{1}{2} \times \frac{1}{2} = \frac{1}{4}$

TH $\frac{1}{2} \times \frac{1}{2} = \frac{1}{4}$

TT $\frac{1}{2} \times \frac{1}{2} = \frac{1}{4}$

The probability of each outcome is written by a branch of the tree

List all of the possible combined outcomes

Calculate the combined probabilities

daydream EDUCATION

75

Expected & Relative Frequency

Expected Frequency

The expected frequency of an outcome of an event, for a specific number of events, can be estimated using the following formula:

Expected frequency = Number of events × Probability of outcome

Ellie rolls a dice 12 times. What is the estimated frequency of her rolling a six?

Probability of rolling a six:

Fraction	Decimal	Percentage
$\frac{1}{6}$	$0.1\dot{6}$	$16.\dot{6}\%$

Expected frequency of rolling a six = $12 \times \frac{1}{6}$
= 2

If the results differ significantly from the expected frequency, it is likely that the event is not "fair". This makes the event biased.

For example, a dice can be weighted so that it lands on one number more than the others.

Relative Frequency

Probability is not always predetermined. For example, in football, a win, lose, and draw are not equally likely. In such situations, probability is estimated using relative frequency.

$$\text{Relative frequency} = \frac{\text{Frequency of outcome}}{\text{Total number of events}}$$

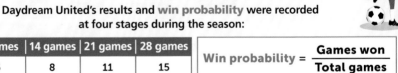

Daydream United's results and **win probability** were recorded at four stages during the season:

Results	7 games	14 games	21 games	28 games
Won	5	8	11	15
Drew	1	2	5	7
Lost	1	4	5	6
P (win)	$\frac{5}{7}$	$\frac{8}{14}$	$\frac{11}{21}$	$\frac{15}{28}$

$$\text{Win probability} = \frac{\text{Games won}}{\text{Total games}}$$

The most precise estimated win probability in the table is $\frac{15}{28}$ because it has been calculated from the largest data set.

In smaller data sets, the chance of anomalies is greater. For example, calculate the win ratio for the season (28 games) based on the win ratio from the team's first seven games.

daydream
EDUCATION

Frequency Tables

A **frequency table** is used to record how often a value (or set of values) occurs. Frequency tables can be arranged in rows or columns. The frequency tables below show the number of computers owned by a group of students.

No. of computers	Frequency
0	0
1	5
2	8
3	7
4	2

No. of computers	0	1	2	3	4
Frequency	0	5	8	7	2

Sometimes, it is easier to count the frequency with a tally, as follows:

No. of computers	0	1	2	3	4
Tally		ЖТ	ЖТ III	ЖТ II	II
Frequency	0	5	8	7	2

Based on the tables above, how many students own two computers?

Grouped Frequency Tables

Grouped frequency tables organise data into intervals and are often used for large data sets. The table below shows the ages of people at a concert.

Age	Frequency
15 ≤ a < 25	4,983
25 ≤ a < 35	5,679
35 ≤ a < 45	3,219
45 ≤ a < 55	1,823
55 ≤ a < 65	946
65 ≤ a < 75	210
Total	**16,860**

The age interval 15 ≤ a < 25 is equal to or greater than 15 and less than 25.

Cumulative Frequency Tables

Cumulative frequency tables keep a running total of the frequencies of a data set. The table below shows the weights of people taking part in a football tournament.

Weight (kg)	Frequency	Cumulative Frequency
50 ≤ w < 55	3	3
55 ≤ w < 60	14	17
60 ≤ w < 65	32	49
65 ≤ w < 70	26	75
70 ≤ w < 75	10	85
75 ≤ w < 80	8	93
80 ≤ w < 85	2	95

The weight interval 50 ≤ w < 55 is equal to or greater than 50 and less than 55.

Displaying Data

Data is a series of observations, facts or statistics. Raw data can be difficult to understand and read. As a result, it is often organised in diagrams, graphs and charts.

Qualitative data is non-numerical data e.g. hair colour.	**Discrete (numerical) data** has specific values e.g. number of cakes sold.	**Continuous (numerical) data** can take any value e.g. height or time.

Bar Charts

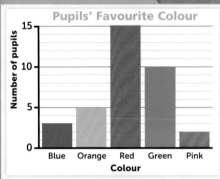

Pupils' Favourite Colour

How many pupils' favourite colour is green?

A bar chart can be used to display qualitative and categorical numerical data. Data is represented using different sized bars. When drawing bar charts:

• Give the graph a title
• Always label both axes
• Use equal intervals on the axes
• Leave a gap between each bar

Bar line graphs use lines instead of bars.

Pictograms

A pictogram uses pictures to represent data. All pictures must be the same.

Pupils' Favourite Ice Cream Flavour

Flavour		Frequency
Chocolate	🍦🍦🍦🍦	16
Vanilla	🍦🍦🍦	10
Strawberry	🍦🍦🍦	12
Mint	🍦	6
Raspberry	🍦	2
Bubble Gum	🍦🍦	8

🍦 = 4 pupils

What is the pupils' favourite ice cream flavour?

Dual Bar Graphs

A dual bar graph displays two sets of data so it is easy to make comparisons.

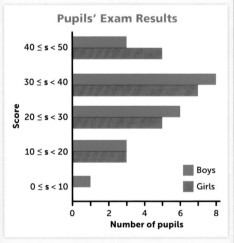

Pupils' Exam Results

Boys
Girls

How many boys scored less than 10 in their exam?

daydream
EDUCATIO

Line Graphs

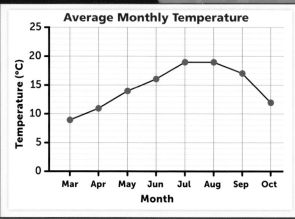

Average Monthly Temperature

In a **line graph**, data is plotted as a series of points that are joined with straight lines.

Line graphs are used to display continuous data and help show trends or change over time.

Always ensure your line graph has a title and that the axes are labelled and at equal intervals.

What was the average monthly temperature in June?

Pie Charts

A pie chart is a circular chart that is split into sections to show proportion. The table below shows pupils' favourite sport. Follow the steps to create a pie chart for this data.

Step 1. In a pie chart, data is represented as a proportion of 360, as there are 360° in a circle. Therefore, to calculate the proportion for each person surveyed, divide 360 by the total number of people surveyed, 360 ÷ 30 = 12.

Sport	Frequency	Frequency × 12	Proportion of 360
Rugby	4	4 × 12 = 48	48
Football	8	8 × 12 = 96	96
Cricket	4	4 × 12 = 48	48
Netball	6	6 × 12 = 72	72
Swimming	3	3 × 12 = 36	36
Tennis	2	2 × 12 = 24	24
Hockey	3	3 × 12 = 36	36
Total	30	30 × 12 = 360	360

Step 2. To calculate the proportions for each sport, multiply their frequencies by 12.

4 × 12 = 48

Step 3. Now that the sports have been converted to proportions of 360, the pie chart can be drawn.

Start by drawing a straight line from the centre of the circle to the edge.

Use a protractor to measure and mark the angles for each sport, and label them accordingly.

Hockey 3

Rugby 4

Tennis 2

36° 48°

Swimming 3

24°

36°

96° Football 8

72°

48°

Netball 6

Cricket 4

Travel Graphs

A distance/time graph is a type of travel graph. Distance is measured up the *y*-axis (vertical) and time is measured along the *x*-axis (horizontal).

Gradient of graph = Speed
The steeper the graph, the faster the speed.

$$\text{Speed} = \frac{\text{Distance}}{\text{Time}}$$

Sections of the graph that slope **upward** from left to right represent distance travelled away from the starting point.	Sections of the graph that slope **downward** from left to right represent distance travelled toward the starting point.

A horizontal line indicates that no distance is being travelled.

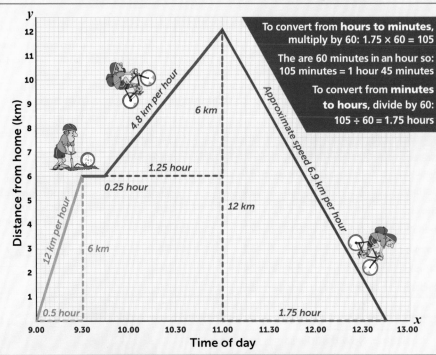

To convert from **hours to minutes**, multiply by 60: 1.75 × 60 = 105

The are 60 minutes in an hour so: 105 minutes = 1 hour 45 minutes

To convert from **minutes to hours**, divide by 60: 105 ÷ 60 = 1.75 hours

Distance from home (km) — *Time of day*

12 km per hour — 0.5 hour — 6 km
0.25 hour
4.8 km per hour — 1.25 hour — 6 km
Approximate speed 6.9 km per hour — 1.75 hour — 12 km

The Story Told by the Graph

- John set off at 9:00. His speed was **12 km/h**: 6 km ÷ 0.5 h = **12 km/h**
- After half an hour, he had a puncture.
  It took **15 minutes** to repair.
- He continued his journey at a slower speed of **4.8 km/h**: 6 km ÷ 1.25 h = **4.8 km/h**
- At **11:00** he started his journey home and arrived at **12:45**.
  His speed was **6.9 km/h**: 12 km ÷ 1.75 h = **6.9 km/h**

Scatter Graphs

Scatter graphs are used to show how closely two sets of data are related. Correlation describes how the two sets of data are related.

Positive Correlation

When the **plotted points** go upward from left to right, there is positive correlation.

As one quantity increases, the other increases. As one quantity decreases, the other decreases.

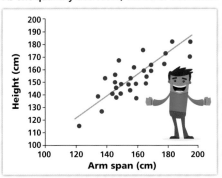

This graph shows that there is positive correlation between height and arm span. As height increases, so does arm span.

Negative Correlation

When the **plotted points** go downward from left to right, there is negative correlation.

As one quantity increases, the other decreases.

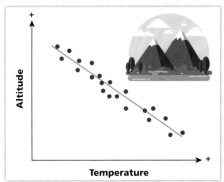

This graph shows that there is negative correlation between altitude and temperature. As altitude increases, temperature decreases.

No Correlation

When there is no linear relationship between two data sets, there is no correlation.

This graph shows that intelligence is not related to shoe size.

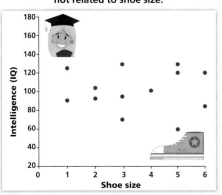

Line of Best Fit

A line of best fit is a line that is drawn through the centre of a group of data points.

When the plotted points are close to the line of best fit, there is **strong correlation**. When they are spread out on either side of the line of best fit, there is **moderate correlation**.

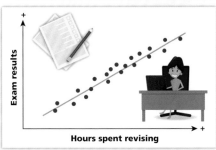

This graph shows a **strong positive correlation**.

Correlation and Causation

A correlation between two variables does not necessarily mean there is a direct cause-and-effect relationship between them.

Example >>> There is a strong positive correlation between number of cars owned and life expectancy. However, these variables are not directly related. Buying more than one car does not increase life expectancy. What other variable could be involved?

Mathematical Formulae

Area of a Rectangle	$A = l \times w$	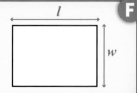 **F**
Area of a Triangle	$A = \frac{1}{2} \times b \times h$	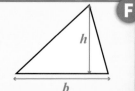 **F**
Area of a Parallelogram	$A = b \times h$	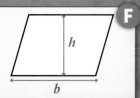 **F**
Area of a Trapezium	$A = \frac{1}{2}(a + b)h$	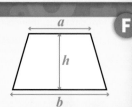 **F**
Circumference of a Circle / **Area of a Circle**	$C = 2\pi r = \pi d$ $A = \pi r^2$	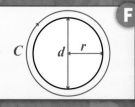 **F**

Volume of a Prism

$V = \textit{area of cross section} \times \textit{length}$

    **F**

daydream EDUCATION